Gorba Oatlands

by

Danny Gill

Copyright © 2015 Georgie Cox

All rights reserved, including the right to reproduce this book, or portions thereof in any form. No part of this text may be reproduced, transmitted, downloaded, decompiled, reverse engineered, or stored, in any form or introduced into any information storage and retrieval system, in any form or by any means, whether electronic or mechanical without the express written permission of the author.

ISBN: 978-1-326-30310-5

Front cover image: Back court, Camden Street.

PublishNation, London
www.publishnation.co.uk

All the proceeds from this book will go to the upkeep of the Southern Necropolis Graveyard on Caledonia Road, Gorbals, Glasgow, Scotland.

My sincere thanks go to all those who purchase this book.

Danny Gill

Foreword

My life growing up in the old tenements in the south side of Glasgow or as we called it the "soo-side" was a magical memory that I will always cherish and fond memories of that great close knit community that we all loved and shared.

Being born just a few years after the end of World War 2, life for all our parents and grandparents was not an easy task but we, the community, all rallied together and shared everything we had. The Gorbals, Laurieston, Hutchensontown and Oatlands all made up the greater Gorbals area and with me being born on the boundary where Oatlands ended and the Gorbals began, I had the joy of not only going to Richmond Park and Shawfield Stadium and the Ritz Picture House nearby too, but also the pleasure of playing with my pals in the Gorbals.

Going to the Gorbals swimming baths and all the many picture houses was a bonus for all us weans, especially the Saturday matinee where we used to watch a great selection of films while cheering on the goodies and booing the baddies, then when the film was over coming out and playing the parts in the streets thinking we were all film stars.

All the neighbours, especially the women, would keep an eye on us weans playing in the streets or back courts as we played games of kick the can or rounders or fitba while the lassies played peever or skipping ropes and growing up in the tenements was a magical experience where every day was like a new adventure.

Most families shared a toilet on the stair head landing and our Ma's took their weekly turn of washing the stairs kneeling down on their hands and knees to do this. Our parents installed into us a set of values to be honest and fair to other people, always help others when you could and most of all to respect our elders, and these set of values have stayed with me all my adult life.

Later on with the Gorbals and Oatlands clearances, most people left the soo-side, shipped out to those new housing schemes on the outskirts of Glasgow be it Castlemilk, Toryglen, Easterhouse or Drumchapel etc and it was here for us, or most of us, for the first time had an inside toilet with the luxury of a bath and a wash hand basin.

This made such a big difference to us because before this our Ma's would put us and our siblings into the old tin bath filled up with boiling water from the kettle on the gas ring and you stood in front of your open coal fire to dry yourself. Later on as we got older in the soo-side our Ma's would give us the money to go and have a hot bath in the Steamie (local wash house).

We had shops everywhere, all along Rutherglen Road, Crown Street and Cumberland Street etc and doing our shopping, or as we called it 'going for the messages' was done on a daily basis as we had no fridges or freezers in those days, it was maybe later in the 1960's we would get tv's and fridges in our tenement house maybe for some people it was later.

See before we had tv's in our houses going for a night out at the picture house was a great event we looked forward to, or maybe a drink in the pub at the weekends for our entertainment, although in the mid to late 1960's the picture houses were changed into bingo halls then sadly that died out too, but we still had our great community spirit. Then as I said, as the Gorbals clearance started, slowly but surely all the people were moving away to the new housing schemes.

It was great having a bath in your house and maybe a wee verandah, you met new friends, but it just wasn't the same as the soo-side where we had an abundance of shops, fish and chip shops, barbers, pubs etc and if we wanted anything to do we had to get a bus back into Glasgow city centre or the Toon as we call it. Above all we didn't have that great community spirit anymore which was really sad.

So in my book here I have tried to recapture and show to the reader by my poems. peoples stories and street songs what our lives were like back in those days, some people stayed in the soo-side and moved into the Dampies and Queen Elizabeth Square which were built to replace the tenements, but they were a structural disaster and within the space of thirty years or so were demolished and with this the last of that community spirit more or less disappeared.

Oh yes we still have the great people of the Gorbals and Oatlands living in their new houses and soo-siders will always be terrific people, but sadly that era of the tenements has gone, although those magic memories will always stay with me till I die. I would also like to leave this book as a legacy to an unborn generation to show them how we lived and got by in those days of the tenements, yes times were hard back then, but I would willingly go back there to live tomorrow if it was possible.

Acknowledgements

I would like to offer my deepest thanks to everyone who has assisted me in the writing of this book, it is truly appreciated. First of all I would like to thank Josephine (Josey) O'Boyle for her tireless work in assisting me in getting everything into the word document typed up and helping me in so many other ways with the book, if it wasn't for Josey's help it would have taken me a considerable time longer to get my book published, so once again thank you very much Josey.

I would also like to thank Norman McNamee, Duncan McCallum, Ronald P A Smith and Glasgow City Council for their kind permission in allowing me the use of their photos for my book, I am indebted to you all and thank you kindly.

My thanks also go to all the people who kindly took time to send me in their stories for my book. I know people must have been getting fed up with all my PM's and emails etc and my posts on Facebook. All your names will appear at the start of you stories and thank you one and all.

I would like to thank Anne McChristie and everyone else who helped me getting the street songs we sang as weans or pointing me in the right direction, thank you all folks.

Many thanks to David and Gwen in Publish Nation who have assisted me in getting my book published, thank you to you both.

I would also like to say thanks to Colin Mackie, his good lady Elsie, Rick Hart and everyone else involved in the upkeep of the Southern Necropolis Graveyard on Caledonia Road in the Gorbals, Glasgow, Scotland and keeping it so neat and tidy. I truly respect all the hard work you all carry out and this is why I'm donating all the proceeds from this book to assist in the upkeep of the Southern Necropolis Graveyard.

CHAPTER 1

Gorbals of the Past

Oh where has the Gorbals gone that we used to love and know,
With its so long hot summers, and its long cauld winters of snow.

Old cobbled streets wae newspaper boys and old shoogly trams,
Wummin aw gaun to the steamie wae their washin in the prams.

Overcrowded tenements but you knew each neighbour's name,
You went away for the "Fair Fortnight" but was glad to get hame.

With a pub on each corner and all your weeks messages on the tic,
Yer Ma took her turn of washin the stairs, even when she wiz sick.

Lassies were aw cawin ropes, while lads played fitba in the street,
Boys got called a Cissy if they skint their knee and started to greet.

Playin games in the Graveyard, hide an seek jist all oot for a laugh,
Come a Friday night yer Mammy would put you in the old tin bath.

So where has the Gorbals gone that we all used to love and know,
I'm afraid it has disappeared my friend, just like Winters cauld snow.

The Single End

We all knew someone who lived there, neighbour, relation or friend,
That wee hoose in the middle of the landing wiz called a Single End.

Was a small dwelling, by health and safety standard we know today,
My wee Granny, Granda and dug lived in wan, only two closes away.

This wee Single End wiz your living room and kitchen, more or less,
Then there was this alcove with a curtain, that was your bed-recess.

A tiny wee lobby wae a coal bunker with door shut to keep oot the dust,
Two chairs and a table in the middle for eating on, always wiz a must.

Aye, the Single End wiz so rare an cosy, the coal fire on so appealing,
Drying your wet clothes on the pulley, that wiz hanging fae the ceiling.

I remember sitting there wae my Granny and listening to her singing,
Then she made us a cup of tea and we done a bit of windae hingin.

The Single Ends have now all gone, but in my mind it's still the same,
That era of our formative years burn on, just like an Eternal Flame.

The Back Court Singer

To the tenements of the soo-side, my memory longs to linger,
Listening to that man who was known as the back court singer.

He'd stand there all unshaven with his auld bunnet in his hand,
Singing his heart out and hoping that a penny soon would land.

Some guy would lift his windae, shout you're doing in my heid,
But a wummin next door took pity, throwing doon a slice o breid.

Singing The Rose of Tralee, ending up with the Skye boat song,
His song list was unendless, in a voice quite wobbly but strong.

So who was this man, and what had happened to him in his life,
Had he once been married with lots of weans and a lovely wife?

It was easy for some people to ignore him while letting out a sigh,
But there for the Grace of our Lord, he could have been you or I.

And as we tell oor grandweans, with amazement they all do look,
Oor back court singer's always remembered in oor history book.

Crown Street

Can it really be almost 70 years ago as my mind goes back so far
There wiz shops as far as your eye could see up past the Hi-Hi Bar.

Gaun fur the messages in Crown St really was a shopper's dream,
Fish and chip shops, butchers/bakers, the Tally's fur an ice cream.

We used to go to the George Cinema, once it wiz called the Crown,
To maybe see a gangster film, or Lauren n Hardy acting the clown.

I recall Stirling Hunter's shop, it sold TV sets maybe small but sleek,
And my Ma went to pay its hire purchase there, every single week.

The Wheatsheaf Pub and the Horseshoe Bar, jist two to name a few,
Where Gorbals men cood have a game of cards as they had a brew.

Hutchesontown Grammar School, with its architectural design so fine,
Doctors' surgeries and Taylor the Dentist, who some called a swine.

The tenements of that era now gone, as people moved far and wide,
But I'll never forget that Crown Street, as its memory burns with pride.

Dizzy Corner

Many's a place in Glesga, where young lovers decided to meet,
But none so famous as Dizzy Corner at Argyle and Union Street.

Young romantics fae the Gorbals, all headed over to the toon,
To stand beneath Boots' Clock, hoping they widdny be let doon.

The lassie wiz standing there aw dressed up like a dugs dinner,
Fur the guy she met at the Plaza, he sure did look like a winner.

Ten feet away stood this guy who kept getting redder in the face,
What if his burd never turned up, that would surely be a disgrace.

But the time wiz now almost eight o'clock, so both were in a tizzy,
Cause they knew within their hearts, both had been given a dizzy.

Gettin a dizzy at Boots' corner, made it never a nice place to be,
I should know whit I'm talking about as it happened 3 times to me.

This all happened in my younger days, I wiz slim wae loads of hair,
Today I only get a dizzy standing up too quick fae my rockin chair.

The Midgie Raker

In the days of the Gorbals old when the tenements did abound,
It was there in the back court that the midgie rakers wiz found.

Now midgie rakin was an art, searching for treasures all hidden,
Wearing short trousers n wellies diving head first into the midden.

But the best of all was young Tommy Kelly and his first cousin Bill,
Who raked aw the soo-side midgies, right up to nearby Govanhill.

Searchin through the middens wiz like gaun through gold coffers,
And when a lucky was found, the shout went up we bags haufers.

They'd rake all day and with their loot they were King of the Castle,
But kept an eye oot fur the polis, who sometimes gave them hassle.

They swapped aw their loot for sweeties with other weans in barter,
Never any flies on the midgie rakers, they didn't come any smarter.

Now their midgie rakin days are all over, they never did see it as a sin,
It's really just as well, cos today how kin ye midgie rake a wheelie bin.

String Wiz The Thing

Don't know the name who invented it but their praises I will so sing,
For everyone from weans to us adults had a good use for auld string.

On the back of our tenement doors with string did hang your key,
Putting your hand through your letter box you got it simple as ABC.

With a hole in two empty tins held by string we pulled with a moan,
Hey Presto us soo-side weans had invented the first mobile phone.

And who can forget the stair head lavvy, newspaper cut in a square,
All tied together with a piece of string as you sat staring into the air.

The midden men were no fools emptying our middens day and night,
To stop rats running up their legs their trews had string pulled tight.

Then when you had the toothache with a terrible pain in your mooth,
Ye tied a bit of string around it and with wan pull oot came the tooth.

It seems to me as I write this poem our memories are a funny thing,
The soo-side would have came to a stop if we didny hiv any string.

Pre-Supermarket Days

Today most of us shop at the supermarket be it instore or online,
How gaun fur the messages differed, for that generation of mine.

See TV it was only a new thing, the internet hiddny been invented,
Nae surfin the net fur a bargain, which leaves us almost demented.

There wiz so many shops in the tenements, we cood take oor pick,
And if yer Ma ran oot o money, ye'd get the messages oan the tic.

Nae supermarkets in those days, nae credit cards to give us a worry,
Ane nae pushin wonky wheeled trolleys roon the aisles in a big hurry.

In the 50's hardly anybody had a fridge, messages got by the hour,
Leavin milk overnight on the windae ledge, hoping it didn't turn sour.

Today when I look at supermarket queues, nae speaking to wan another,
So different from years gone by when gaun fur messages fur my Mother.

Aye online shopping is the thing today, supermarkets on every street,
As I think back to years ago when gaun fur the messages wiz a treat.

Washin the Stairs

This weekly chore in the tenements wiz done with lovin care,
When your Ma or the neighbour took turns to wash the stair.

Now oor Mas had it timed all to perfection, to do their chore,
The weans at school, postman's been, into the stair she tore.

The stairs at first got a sweep, so no dust wiz a laying there,
Then with a pail of hot soapy watter your Ma washed the stair.

On hands and knees your Mammy knelt, working like a navvy,
Making the stairs spotless, especially round the stairheid lavvy.

Each side of the stair got pipe chalked to a dead brilliant white,
When they were finished oor tenement stairs looked a delight.

But if yer Ma was taken ill and her outlook wizny lookin dreamy,
She still took her turn otherwise she'd be the talk o the steamie.

This was the tenement I grew up in closing my eyes they thrive,
And wish to God I was back there cause my Ma would be alive.

The Hoat Watter Boattle

Winter times could be freezing, in the tenements of old,
As the windaes rattled with the wind it made you so cold.

Sitting round the fireside while listening to the radio or TV,
You'd feel so very cosy in fact as snug as a bug could be.

Then your ma would say it's time for bed and off you'd go,
And in an emergency you knew under the bed wiz the po.

Earlier your hoat watter boattle had been filled by Ma's hand,
Wrapping a jumper around it to make your bed feed grand.

First thing you did when in bed, was touch it with your feet,
But quickly drew them back because of that bloomin heat.

Then when your feet wiz warm you cuddled the boattle tight,
And drifted off to slumber the winter stars shining so bright.

Today we hiv electric blankets, central heating at full throttle,
But I don't half miss the tenements and my hoat watter boattle.

Gaun Tae The Dentist

Dentists all over the soo-side, their names all filled me with dread,
Laying back in their chair terrified, with that drill jist over your head.

He'd get his long handled mirror so to hiv a good look in yer mooth,
Saying there's nothing else fur it, I'll have to pull out your bad tooth.

Clamping on that gas mask, he told ye count back to 10 real slow,
But the most I ever reached was 7, then off to sleep I would go.

When you woke up you'd be a bit groggy, yer heid a spinning roon,
Handing you a glass of pink mouthwash, you'd spit into the spitoon.

Then the gas mask got replaced by a needle, injected into yer gum,
Half of your face wiz freezing, yer mouth was feeling pure dead numb.

If ye had a filling and the drill hit the nerve, you jumped up intae the air,
With a scarf tied around your mooth, you ran doon that bloomin stair.

Now as I get near to seventy years old, every day I seem so humbler,
Dentists don't worry me cause at night my dentures go into a tumbler.

Times Gone By

Oh where has the soo-side gone that we all knew as young weans,
Travelling intae the Central or St Enoch's by steam engined trains.

Remember as a 14 year old watchin last night of the Glasgow Trams,
Ma and other wummin gaun tae the steamie with washin in the prams.

Gaun fur a day in Richmond Park, aye those days were a great thrill,
Raking the midgies in the soo-side, the lucky wans up in Govanhill.

Looking forward to seeing the pictures, the matinees were a big treat,
Cheering on the goodies, and booing the baddies, life was so sweet.

Runnin fur a message to the shops, then play a game o kick the can,
In the water at Gorbals swimming baths then aff to the Hot Peanut Man.

Boys playin fitba, lassies playin peever, with a nice ribbon in their hair,
Fish n chips on a Friday, Glasgow Green to see the shows at the fair.

Then the Gorbals clearance, so we moved to housing schemes so vast,
Nae mair dreepin aff dykes or the Venny, oor memories will always last.

Pre-Mobile Phone Days

It seems everyone has a mobile phone today but it wasn't always so,
They hadn't been invented, when I wiz a wean over sixty years ago.

We had telephone boxes in the street, painted a coloured bright red,
Which had an 'A' and a 'B' button, and into four old penny's you fed.

Then in the tenements of the late 1950's life wiz really looking fine,
Some soo-side people got a phone, even though it wiz a party line.

So, now with a phone in the hoose, we could phone up oor pals at will,
You would gab for ages and stuff the cost until Ma and Da got the bill.

We were moving with the times and things wur changing so very quick,
When all of a sudden we had a mobile phone the size of a house brick.

But as time moved on, new mobile phones fitted into all of oor pockets,
If Granny wiz alive to see all this her eyes would pop oot their sockets.

Looking back I think folk were happier before mobiles were all invented,
Cause with all the new apps we are getting, I'm mobile phone demented.

School Summer Holidays

Let's go for a walk doon memory lane when the sun shone unrelented,
It was oor school summer holidays and we ran about pure demented.

No more school for 6 or 7 weeks, every morning we rose wae the lark,
Jeely pieces wrapped in newspaper, as we headed fur Richmond Park.

The space race had started, monkeys in rockets flying roon the moon,
Bill Hayley wiz rockin aroon the clock as Elvis made aw the girls swoon.

Those summer school holidays fur us weans really wiz a magic dream,
Oor ma's gave us money for a poke of chips or a MaCallums ice cream.

Every day was an adventure day jumping fae dyke to dyke jist fur a dare,
Some of us went doon to Saltcoats fur 2 weeks, it was the Glasgow Fair.

We held fitba matches against the weans next street hopin no to get beat,
Older weans took a trip over to the toon, visiting Lewis's in Argyle Street.

Lassies holding a concert in oor back courts, aw winners, naebody losers,
I'll never forget that summer holiday wae a snake belt roon mah troosers.

The Clelland Bar

Let's take a trip down memory lane to the corner of Hospital/Ballater St,
For there stood the Clelland Bar, and it's music lounge coodny be beat.

Along with my girlfriend we went there, with other couples in oor throngs,
To listen to the live music bands playing, all the hit of the day pop songs.

There was also a public bar where you drank a pint and all had the craic,
Where the supporters coach took us to the match, then dropped us back.

In the music lounge it wiz all table service, cos it wiz all packed to the hilt,
All the Clelland barmaids were immaculate wearing a beautiful tartan kilt.

The Clelland wiz pure dead magic, it wiz the best of all the Gorbals bars,
As the band belted out Tom Jones' "Delilah" of Engelbert's "Ten Guitars."

This was the sexy swinging sixties, and I always went there every week,
The Mersey Beat wis all the rage, the Rollin Stones were at their peak.

Then the Gorbals clearance, the tenements and the Clelland disappeared,
But I'll never forget that lounge where we sat, drank, clapped and cheered.

Rutherglen Road

At Jenny's Burn in Oatlands where the smell it wasn't so sweet,
Started Rutherglen Rd going all the way over to Gorbals Street.

It passed by Richmond Park and nearby Hutchie Bowling Green,
Passing the Ritz picture hoose where many a good film was seen.

Then meandering past McNeil St, where the library once stood,
Where as a wean I borrowed books, the reading wiz oh so good.

Then Greasy Peter's Chippy, nearby Dirty Maggie's Comic Shop,
And along Rutherglen Rd tenements the 101 trolley bus did stop.

This is the road I used to walk to get to Gorbals swimming baths,
Schools off of the side streets where we all got taught our maths.

Next wiz the Rose Garden/Twomax's sewing factory using cotton,
Florence St where Benny Lynch was born, he'll never be forgotten.

Coming next to Crown St with shops and pubs we really had a load,
Finally coming to Gorbals Street, where ended old Rutherglen Road.

The Cumbie

There were many gangs in Glesga, Brigton Derry, Tongs or the Fleet,
But the wan I remember best came fae all around Cumberland Street.

They were known as The Cumbie, most went to Big Bonnie's School,
And if you went to fight them, then you were either a bampot or a fool.

The Glasgow Constabulary branded them a terror to all of the nation
That's why the polis locked themselves in to Lawmoor Police Station

You had the Cumbie, Young Young Cumbie, and the Tiny Cumbie Crew,
Not forgetting all the lassies who were members of the She-Cumbie too

The Cumbie were hard street fighters, their reputation was oh so mean,
I saw them fightin a few times when the shows were at Glasgow Green.

The Cumbie wiz a symptom of our streets, it's not meant to sound crass,
And as they ran into battle, their cry was a scream of "Cumbie Ya Bass!"

Now as the auld Cumbie members mellow and aren't anymore touchy,
I still canny forget those battles they had with the Young Young Hutchie.

New Years Past

Hogmanay in the tenements is a time that I will always treasure,
Ma had scrubbed the weans and hoose spotless to her pleasure.

There was whiskey and sherry in bottles, just sitting on the table
And enough shortbread and currant bun to eat if you were able.

We sat and watched Andy Stewart on TV singing all of his songs,
Glaswegians stood in George Square waitin fur the bells to bong.

We wished each other Happy New Year in the future many more,
While waiting for oor first footer to walk through oor opened door.

They'd bring in their own bottle, to pour you a hauf, or maybe two,
Us weans would be sitting under the kitchen table drinking Irn-Bru.

Then with your hoose full of neighbours, ne'erday wiz in full blast
Folks taking a turn to sing that's how I remember new years past.

The soo-side of auld has gone I know, but I remember it so clear,
As I Danny Gill wish you all my friends a Happy Good New Year.

Eglinton Street

From the Laurieston Bar at Bridge St right up to Eglinton Toll,
Here stands Eglinton Street that once had tenements with soul.

You had many shops, public houses and Churches of Glory,
Having a pint in the Mally Arms listening to the barman's story.

The railway line to the Central Station taking folk tae the toon,
Wan o the few things the Gorbals clearance diddny bring doon.

Sadly those shops have gone that we knew in Eglinton Street,
No more Hell's Kitchen Cafe for a cup of tea and sumthin to eat.

I wiz told I'd see big changes, the tenements have gone away,
In their place I jist couldn't believe it, was part of the motorway.

Gaun to the Coliseum or Bedford flicks for the matinee pictures,
Sittin their eyes glued to the screen with a bag of dolly mixtures.

The Eglinton Street that we once knew is now only in imagination,
All has nearly been demolished, except Bridge St Subway Station.

Paddy's Market

Paddy's Market wiz always packed, with a buzz always in the air,
In fact it got that busy, you'd swear blind half of Glesga wiz there.

Gorbals folks walked over the Albert Bridge across the River Clyde,
All looking fur a cheap bargain as us soo-siders stood side by side.

There wiz auld tin baths, second hand tools laying there all asunder,
Auld tackity boots and shoes wae no laces, all for 6d or even under.

Old fur coats at a bargain price, old clothes piled up three feet high,
I tell ye there wiz hardly anything in Paddy's Market you coodny buy.

A cafe nearby selling ribs and cabbage or big plate of stewed beef,
And a big mug of extra strong tea wid strip the enamel aff yer teeth.

But then Glasgow City Council shut Paddy's Market, we were so irate,
Jist as well we still hiv the Barras, a wee bit alang the auld Gallowgate.

And although Paddy's Market has gone, we all remember it wae pride,
Cos many's a bargain went back wae us tae the hoose in the soo-side.

Fridays

When I was young all those years ago, Fridays were beyond compare,
Cause my wage packet was all in cash, tonight I would be a millionaire.

Everyone was happy that day and finishing time coodny come too soon,
After paying your housekeeping to your Ma, you headed over the toon.

It wiz Friday night and you had just been paid, spending with no regrets,
The fags you smoked during the week, changed fur American cigarettes

You met up with your pals in a pub o'er the toon, fur a right good swally,
Everybody had loads of cash, drinking quickly and all getting quite pally.

Then it wiz decision time, which hall would it be fur the Friday dancing,
At times I'd go to the Plaza, but Barrowland was better fur romancing.

And if I got a lumber then I would gladly escort the lassie hame alright,
If the winching wiz good, then we'd make a date for the following night.

Aye Friday nights were so brilliant, spending oor money without disdain,
And if I was skint on a Sunday, then it was only 5 days to Friday again.

Caledonia Road

From the old Ritz picture hoose, where many's a good film showed,
Right down to Thomson's Greek Church in Hospital St ran Cally Rd.

Opposite the Ritz wiz the Coronation Bar, frequented by a good few,
Along a wee bit stood St Bonaventure's Church where I took a pew.

Facing St Bonnie's a row of cottages then the Southern Necropolis,
With many a poor soul resting there, in Glasgow's mighty metropolis.

All along Cally Road you'd streets all heading down to the River Clyde,
This wiz the time when the tenements stood, covering all the soo-side.

I walked along the Cally Rd when I was jist a wean in short troosers,
We had newsagents, fish and chip shops and many a wee boozers.

In the 60's and 70's the landscape changed, was it Labour or the Tories,
The Cally Rd we all knew got rebuilt wae maisonettes and multi-storeys.

Everyone has their memories of Cally Rd, different era's and phases,
Who can forget the night getting lit wae the sparks fae Dixon's Blazes.

Polmadie Road

This thoroughfare starts at Rutherglen Rd, jist at Richy Park,
Where Oatlands folks over the years were happy as a lark.

Wolseley and Roseberry Streets crossed over in a straight line,
The Splash and Molls Mire pubs, for you and me were so fine.

With Roseberry Park Juniors playing football with a strict code,
Toryglen St where Glen Daly also dwelt, was off Polmadie Rd.

Then you had St Margaret's Church, with stonework quite neat,
Almost beside it you had the Pen leading on to Elmfoot Street.

After passing Kilbride Street was an industrial estate to the right,
And at Polmadie Locomotive Shed engines did all berth at night.

While in summer nights of lightness, or the winter nights of dark,
Football fans in their thousands marched up to Hampden Park.

Now Polmadie Road is not mentioned much which it's sad to say,
But it's still a vital link in Oatlands, as I write my wee poem today.

Logan Street

The Logan Bar was a busy pub where Oatlands folk did meet,
It wiz on the corner of Rutherglen Road and also on Logan St.

Opposite wiz Deefy McGreegor's shop with his dug so big n lazy,
Cause he wiz deef you had to shout and the alsation went crazy.

Just up fae Deefy's you had a Bookmakers shop only yards away,
Gambling was illegal then, and the polis took the punters all away.

Just roon the corner wiz wee Jeannie French's shop sellin sweets,
And many's a time Logan St weans went in there for penny treats.

Who can forget Wolseley St School, where you never made a fuss,
Every day learning your lessons, hoping to pass your eleven plus.

Those one storey houses going down to Kilbride St oh so very neat,
Lassies playing peever, boys playing "fitba"; all the length of Logan St.

Yet the Logan St that my generation knew, is now sadly of the past,
But growing up there in Oatlands fifty years ago really it wiz a blast.

Last Day at School

Who remembers that last day at school, do you remember it well?
Counting down the seconds 'til the teacher rang the 4 o'clock bell.

So many in schools in Glasgow, especially our own loved soo-side,
Did you go to Bonnie's, Bosco or Adelphi, near to the River Clyde.

Whatever school attended, our teachers and lessons were a blast,
But this would soon be history, as today at school wiz yer very last.

So how did you feel on your last day, walking through that old gate?
No more to be reprimanded, if you happened to be five minutes late.

Wanting my last day special, I went to Tam Shepherds' Joke Shop,
Got the bus back to Holyrood and six stink bombs I surely did drop.

I let them off in my last lesson, the teacher cried out What a smell!
Everyone said it was Danny Gill Sir, but I was saved by the last bell.

People always remember man walking on the moon, it was so cool,
But coodny compare with the elation I felt at my last day at school.

First Day at Work

Was your first day at work a pleasure or like mine, a bit of a disaster,
As I started out in life to work with face bricks, concrete and plaster.

On my first day I stood at Clyde St/Saltmarket in the year of 1963,
The van picked up all the waiting men, but without picking up me.

The boss forgot to tell the driver, the new boy would be at the drop,
My Ma phoned him up and I spent my first day at the Joiner's Shop.

So that's how my first day at work started, didn't cover myself in glory,
But I'm sure that everyone reading this poem has his/her own story.

Was your first day at work a good wan or like me did ye feel let doon,
Maybe your job wiz in a new factory, or bank or a shop over the toon.

Did you get sent fur a tin of tartan paint, so much to your total dismay,
Or get sent fur a long staun and you were staunin there all o' the day.

My last day at school and my first day at work, I remember them well,
And I am so glad that my memories to others I can always happily tell.

The Venny

Memories for us Gorbals weans are all very plentiful and so many,
It was helped to be built by weans themselves calling it The Venny.

Actually there were two Vennys built, one after the other in phases,
The first one close to Gorbals St, the other near to Dixon's Blazes.

What an adventure playground they were, dead brilliant and grand,
Who cared if we ripped oor clothes, or got a big skelf into the hand.

Rope ladders, tyre swings, shoogly platforms and a climbing frame,
Or zip wire we called The Flying Fox, we never wanted to go hame.

Health and safety would not have it today, it wouldn't stand a hope,
Especially with twenty weans together, swinging on the Tarzan rope.

The people in charge took us off camping to Arran, it really wiz a joy,
Or to the Campsies or Balquhidder which holds the grave of Rob Roy.

Thinking back to that time, skint knees, bruised shins and other pains,
I'm glad to say we played in the Venny, when we were Gorbals weans.

The Newspaper

Buying the newspaper in Glasgow kept us up with the news and times,
Pat Roller fae the Daily Record kept his eyes oot for any street crimes.

But newspaper sheets had many other uses, needs were demanding,
Oor Ma's cut it into wee squares for in the cludgie on the stair landing.

Then what aboot the tenement, coal fire lightin it could be a real caper,
To get the fire started, over the opening you held a sheet o newspaper.

Oh we loved that open fire, the heat was magic, I'm really no kiddin,
Last night's ashes got wrapped in newspaper, dumped in the midden.

And when it was raining oor soaking wet footwear gave us aw the blues,
We'd shove newspaper in them overnight, then we had bone dry shoes.

Remember a Friday night getting a fish supper wrapped in newspaper,
Shoving it up yer jumper to keep it hot, smelling aw that vinegar vapour.

So many thanks to the newspaper industry my blessings are so profuse,
For us canny soo-siders put your newspaper to many's a very good use.

Queen Lizzie Flats

Who can forget the Queen Lizzie flats built with concrete so dense,
Gorbals folk never will or their Architect, the bampot, Basil Spence.

Standing there twenty stories high people said it took some beating,
First time we had a bath of our own, and under floor central heating.

At first folks had to queue up, to put their name down for these flats,
Leaving behind the tenements and the back courts, puddles and rats.

Do you remember standin at ground level at those big concrete feet?
It was like a wind tunnel, and you could be blown over to Ballater St.

Verandas at each end of the block, to dry skirts, troosers and blouses,
The lift halted every second floor to let us into our maisonette houses.

Then after a decade of dampness, all our dreams turned to sad tears,
Tried to refurbish them, but had to demolish them, after only 30 years.

And on the day of demolition, an awful tragedy occurred with sad regret,
Mrs Tinney sadly lost her life and this Gorbals people will never forget.

The Co-op Dividend Number

Can you remember the Co-op of all those years gone by so long,
You got messages fur yer Ma, and never got the number wrong.

Your Ma told you her Divvy number from when you were a wean,
It wiz drilled into your memory and forever imprinted in your brain.

You first heard your Ma's number, as she rattled it off with pride,
As she dragged you to every Co-op shop, in the whole soo-side.

And I remember standing in the Co-op, as the money wiz put in a cup,
As it whizzed its way to the cashier, seated in the office way high up.

The Divvy pay-oot was fantastic and you got it paid oot every year,
Made your Ma dead happy, buying all her weans tons of new gear.

Ma's Divvy number still gets used each week, but in a different way,
The numbers I use for the lottery and hope I'll be lucky some day.

When we meet Saint Peter at the Pearly Gates, he'll say wae a grin.
If you canny remember yer Ma's divvy number, yer jist no getting in.

Your Trusted Wellies

Pullin oan yer trusted wellies, and runnin doon the tenement stair,
Gaun intae the back court as all yer wee pals were playing there.

It wiz rainin the night before, all the puddles were full up of watter,
And jumpin in with your wellies oan, yer pals diddny half all scatter.

In the summer time you wore sandals or American baseball boots,
But I wiz always happy with my trusty wellies on to cover my toots.

Us soo-side weans wore oor wellies without a single sign of abash,
Only thing wiz they rubbed on your legs so ye got the soo-side rash.

Jumpin in the puddles yer clothes got wet, you never had any shame,
Until yer Ma screamed at you, Just you wait til yer faither gets hame.

For puddle splashin wellies were great, but no good to ride a bike,
And your feet would keep on slipping if ye tried tae climb up a dyke.

All good memories, but now I'm a pensioner with my aches n pains,
And I love to think back to when we were all soo-side wellie weans.

Eglinton Toll

How many times have we all passed it by bus or gaun fur a stroll,
Its proper name is St Andrew's Cross, but we call it Eglinton Toll.

Met my pals on Friday as weans gaun to Crossmyloof Ice Rink,
Later in years I met the same pals but we went fur a wee drink.

Up Vicky Road you'd the Odeon Cinema, later was the Cinerama,
Saw many a film in there, Cowboy, Gangster, or mibby a drama.

Then doon a wee bit wiz the Plaza, for all oor weekend dancing,
Everybody all dressed up to their nines for a bit of "romancing."

With McNee's pub next door, you walked in cool as a cucumber,
But only had wan drink, as in the Plaza you might get a lumber.

Now sadly these buildings are gone, sad but it's the God's truth,
And with all of their demolition, went the best years of my youth.

But jist a minute, haud yer horses, the Star Bar is still at the Toll,
Where ye kin get a 3 course meal or a plate of soup with a roll.

Ballater Street

Where hiv all the tenements gone, it makes you want to greet,
In your memory you see them all, and yer pals in Ballater St.

Who remembers Greens Playhouse and the Soo-side Sawmills?
The Clelland Bar wae music, pints of heavy and quarter of gills.

Waddell Street and Commercial Road their tenements now gone by,
Ballater Street has all new houses and tower blocks up in the sky.

You had the UCBS Bakery and St Mungo's Halls built oh so well,
The Bonded Warehouse, who wid ever forget, that whiskey smell.

Seems like only yesterday I saw trolley buses, shoogley trams,
As they passed me by, and wummin with weans in their prams.

The Cumbie fought The Tongs at the Spenny Bridge wae severity,
And chased them away fur daring to invade the Gorbals territory.

It seems like a life time ago, but our memories still remain sweet,
Oor community spirit 'twas unbreakable in the likes of Ballater St.

The Laurieston Bar

There's a pub standing on Bridge St, it's called The Laurieston Bar,
And everyone who drinks there say it's the best pub around by far.

It's run by the Clancy family and their aim is always to please,
The drink it is fantastic and for a snack you have pie an peas.

There's lots of pictures on the walls of the old Gorbals in its prime,
When you stand and look at them, you're transported back in time.

John Clancy does the morning, while brother James does the night,
With sister Ann and Joe and Mark, your drinks are always dead right.

Sitting in the lounge bar with the decor so sixties and very proud,
Usually it's so quiet till you get a visit from the Sub Crawl Crowd.

The range of beers are so many, it really is a touch of class,
And the Clancy's pour your pint from a fridge pre-chilled glass.

Yes the Laurieston Bar in the Gorbals, will never ever let you down,
And I'll be heading for there, when I'm back home in Glasgow town.

Richmond Park

Who can remember Richy Park before it had houses on it built,
Well I hope Glasgow City Council does as it must share its guilt.

Remember the summer holidays, off to the Richy, you and me,
After passing the Sonny Pon, we'd all spit at the Old Devil's Tree.

First we'd go to the rockery, then to the swing park with a hoot,
Climbing the monkey bars, using greasy paper on the big chute.

Then we went to see the swans as they swam through ra watter,
Or tried to fish Baggie Minnies, but the net jist made them scatter.

Aye those were the days so long ago, the park was always clean,
And for two old pennies you could play golf, on the putting green.

Was a great day oot fur Gorbals weans, and new pals you'd meet,
Oatlands people diddny hiv too far to go, just walk over the street.

But no matter how many hooses were built by Architects so clever,
They'll never erase oor memories, it's the Richy Park for us forever.

CHAPTER 2

Danny Gill

I was born in the Southern General Hospital on 11th of January 1948 and was brought up in number 40 Fauldhouse Street, Oatlands (almost at the boundary where Oatlands ended and the Gorbals began).

My ma, da and big sister Jeanette were living in 2 Snowdon Street, Gorbals but when I was on the way, ma and da decided to move to Fauldhouse Street as it was a bigger place - a room and kitchen. It was in the tenements with no inside toilet and like thousands of other people living in the tenements we shared a stair head landing toilet with other families. There was something magic about the tenement buildings in the soo-side as we had this unbreakable community spirit with everyone knowing each other and granny's and granda's and uncles and aunts all living close by or maybe only a few streets away.

Being born and brought up in Oatlands just a few years after the end of World War 2, life was very austere for everybody and money was very tight all around - I think that this was what brought all of us together, we might not have had much but what we did have we all shared.

There were things like a "Menage" where our mothers paid in say two shillings and sixpence every week for twelve weeks and then when it was their "turn" to collect the menage money your ma would have money to buy her children clothes or other essentials, and of course for us weans it was great because your ma would always make a fuss over you and buy some sweeties, so us weans loved that.

It was the same when the gas man came to empty our gas meter, all the coins from the wee box where we dropped money in was emptied onto the kitchen table, and the gas man gave your ma a rebate so once again us weans got a penny or two for sweeties that was magic !!.

In our street was the wash-house or as we called it "The Steamie" where our ma's went to wash and dry all their laundry. It was very hard for our mothers and grannies but remember in the 1950's there was no such thing as a washing machine etc in our houses that we take for granted nowadays and our ma's would work like demons slaving in the very hot steamie, then, when it was all done they would pile all their washing into a pram and wheel it along the street until they came to their close-mouth entrance to their tenement or as we called it the "close." Once there, they would then have to bump the pram all the way up the stairs until they came to their own door.

In addition, in the Steamie you had the Hot Baths upstairs. You paid for your hot bath downstairs and got your ticket and towel and a cake of carbolic soap. You went upstairs (usually on a Friday night for most people) and sat on a bench until the man in charge would shout "Next" then you would go in as the guy had poured the hot water into your bath with a turnkey from outside of your cubicle. Once you were in the bath, this guy would then shout out more hot water or cold water and you usually asked for cold, then that was it, he would never give you any more hot or cold water. When you finished you stood on a wooden duck-board drying yourself with the flimsy towel you had hired from downstairs but boy oh boy did you feel good. This made such a change from when we were really small weans and our ma's would shove you and your siblings one at a time into an old tin bath and fill it up with boiling water from the kettle, so it was a sure sign you were getting older when your ma gave you money for a hot bath in the Steamie.

All us weans played so many street games like kick the can, rounders, lassies playing peever/hopscotch or using skipping ropes while all of us boys played football from the moment we got out of school and sometimes it could end up fifteen or twenty a side as we all thought we were either Celtic or Rangers players. These football matches could last for hours on end and sometimes it was one street playing another street.

In those far off days we didn't have video games or lap top computers as children of today have and we made our own entertainment in the streets or the back courts of the tenements like "dreepin aff dykes" (dropping/climbing up/down on the walls separating different back courts) or playing marbles or "jorries" as we called them. Life everyday for us weans in the soo-side was an adventure and we would go "midgie raking," that was looking and searching into the open dustbins but we always called them middens or midgies. It wasn't unknown for us weans to walk for miles to see if we could find any treasures people had thrown into their middens. In the back court tenements of say Govanhill, where at that time some people living there were known as toffs.

I used to love going over to Richmond Park on Rutherglen Road where you had a swing park, a rockery, a golf putting green and a small pond where swans swam and you could fish for "baggy minnies," tiny little fish, I think their proper names are minnows. You would buy a wee fishing net from a shop opposite Richmond Park and take an empty jam jar with you from your house to put your baggy minnies in, but if you did catch any you would keep them for only a day or two then usually you got fed up with them and your ma would tell you to either give them away or get rid of them. Not only weans from Oatlands went to the park but weans from the Gorbals and Bridgeton too and it was like an oasis to everybody who went there. Later on people would sail model boats in the pond and there was also little paddle boats you could hire and enjoy yourself, it was such a great place to go.

As I said earlier that being born on the boundary where Oatlands ended and the Gorbals began, I spent just as much time in the Gorbals as I had wee pals that lived in Moffat Street and Norfolk Street and oh yes, the Gorbals swimming baths it was great going there. I always remember when I was just learning to swim in there that I was walking past the deep end and this boy pushed me in. I went down and was actually drowning until the pool attendant saw what had happened and dived in and saved me, thank God.

After we had finished our allotted time in the Gorbals swimming baths we would walk along to Cleland Street and go to the hot peanut man and get a bag of hot peanuts or maybe a a bit of tablet (our ma's had give us the money for this as well as the swimming money), or maybe we would walk along Rutherglen Road to 'Greasy Peter's Fish and

Chip Shop' and get threepence worth of scrapings which were the leftovers after frying, and they tasted oh so good. When I close my eyes I can still taste them.

I went to 'Wee Bonnies' (Saint Bonaventure's Primary School] and to be truthful, I didn't really like school that much. I just wanted to play football at playtime with all my other school pals. We did however have a great teacher called Mr Jimmy D'Arcy who was always cracking jokes and one of the things he said that I always remember is, "Right boys and girls, I have just found out a great way of getting into the pictures (cinema) without paying." We all said "What's that Sir?" and he replied "Just walk in backwards and they'll think you're going out!!!!") I left 'Wee Bonnies' in 1959 and went to 'Big Bonnies' (the secondary school] for a year but because I was top of the class with great exam marks I was sent to Holyrood Senior Secondary School and stayed there till I was 15 years old then left school without any qualifications at all.

In the mid 1950's we had great music and I always remember us kids loving Bill Hayley and the Comets singing 'Rock Around The Clock' then a new guy called Elvis Presley landed on the scene and music for us changed forever. I remember one summer night in the back courts of the tenements, some girls were standing singing on the top of one of the concrete roofs of a midden, a 'cat's choir' we called it. Anyway they were singing a Buddy Holly song called 'Oh Boy' and they were brilliant and that memory has stayed with me all of my life. This was just another example of us soo-side weans making our own entertainment in the back courts and streets of the Gorbals and Oatlands.

I used to love going with my ma and granny to walk along Cumberland Street with all its many shops, there was always a buzz about Cumberland Street and I have many happy memories about it. However, I also have a very sad memory as my Granda Hendry dropped down dead in front of me and my Granny Hendry as were looking into one of the shop windows in Cumberland Street. My granda and me had been playing football with an empty matchbox only minutes earlier in Caledonia Road. This is another memory that has never left me all of my life, it was so sad, especially as I was only 7 years old.

St Francis Church was a magnificent building and although I attended Mass in St Bonaventure's Church, I went to St Francis' a few times and it was so beautiful in there with a magnificent altar.

I would always go for messages (shopping) to the shops for my ma and if a neighbour wanted a message got for them, they would only have to ask you and you gladly did it, and sometimes they gave you a penny for going for that message for them (but your mammy would always tell you not to take any money for going for messages).

In those days of the tenements shops we bought our food on a daily basis as none of us in the 1950's had fridges to keep food stored in, and it was common practice to leave your milk bottle on the outside window sill overnight and hoping the milk wouldn't curdle. Your ma would always take her turn of washing the stairs and all our windows and net curtains were spotlessly clean, we might not have had much money but we prided ourselves in being clean, honest people and we always showed respect for our elders. This too has stayed with me all of my adult life.

I remember coming home from school when I was 13 years old and the back of our tenement had collapsed due to subsidence, and were moved out to one of the new housing schemes that were getting built all over Glasgow at that time. We moved to South Nitshill and I absolutely hated leaving the soo-side, I kept going back to see my auld pals. This South Nitshill had hardly any shops and we had to travel by bus back into Glasgow if we wanted to go to the dancing or cinema etc. I did meet new pals in South Nitshill, but it just wasn't the same as the soo-side and we had lost that wonderful community spirit.

I went back to the soo-side for drinking in the pubs at the weekends when I was a young man and would have a drink in the 'Mally Arms,' 'Granite City' and most of all the 'Clelland Bar' with my girlfriend Rena Smith at the weekends, for the music lounge and all those great groups and singers. I also went back to Oatlands a few times and had a few pints in the 'Glue Pot Bar,' 'The Braehead Bar,' which were both on Braehaed Street, 'The Roseberry' which was on the corner of Fauldhouse Street and Rutherglen Road, 'Logans Bar' which was on the corner of Logan Street and Rutherglen Road, opposite Richmond Park and the 'Molls Mire' pub on Polmadie Road.

When I was 20 years old and had completed my 5 year apprenticeship as a bricklayer, I left Glasgow in 1968 to build bricks halfway round the world never to return to Glasgow to live (sadly) and only to visit ma, da and sister. I went back to visit the soo-side for the first time in 45 years just a few years ago and when I saw that all the tenements had been demolished I actually felt like greetin. I stood outside of Hutchensontown Bowling Green and looked over to where Fauldhouse Street, 'Big Bonnies' and the Steamie had once stood and I got a lump as big as football in my throat, and there were tears in my eyes thinking back to my parents, grandparents and all the great times of my upbringing. It was really an emotional moment for me to think of that great community spirit we all had and shared, yes we might not have had much money, but to sum life up in those days:-

We had nothing but we had everything.

Peter Mortimer

I was born in the bed recess at 437 Ballater Street in a tenement sometimes known as the 'distillery building', and as you've probably guessed it was on the same block as the Long John distillery. The process of making whisky leaves me with one of my most abiding memories of those days......the smell. The distillery belched out smoke with a unique aroma, of grain and water making the magic golden liquid, and filling the nostrils of everyone in the district. Many people in the Gorbals and beyond hate the smell, but for me it was comforting and homely. I remember the big grain lorries delivering into the Adelphi Street gate, and inevitably some of the little pellets of grain would spill on to the street, only to be snatched up by passing pigeons. The same aroma can still be sniffed, as the distillery continues its production, and any time I'm back in the vicinity it immediately takes me back to my childhood days.

But there was another smell very close by, that I'm sure everyone loved, the mouth watering aroma of bread being made at the nearby UCBS bakery in McNeill Street. It employed around a thousand people and produced bread on an industrial scale, and the vivid memory of their delivery vans parked on the pavement, and workers with bogeys trundling across McNeill Street to load bread, cakes and tea-bread, to be delivered round the many Co-op shops in the city. My oldest brother was known to pilfer from the parked vans.

Across the road from our tenement, the UCBS had a row of shops, which still remain. It was here that they had their 'shan shop' where day old produce, not sold round their shops in the city, was brought to be sold off at knock down prices. I can honestly say I don't know how I would have survived childhood without the 'shanny'. Like most Gorbals mothers, my wee Maw faced a constant struggle to feed us, and more often than not, me and my older brother would return home at dinner time from Hayfield Primary School to a cup of tea and a couple of buns. It was back to school before coming home at 4.00 pm with our dinner around an hour later. The 'shan shop' was very basic and no frills, about four or five women, dressed in white overalls and wee hats, sold off the past its best produce, which ranged from bread and cakes, to buns and the like. My brother was usually sent across the street for 6d worth of buns and told to avoid a certain assistant in the 'shanny' as she was less than generous when she filled the bag with her interpretation of sixpence worth.

The struggle to make ends meet for my wee Maw inevitably involved taking my Da's suit to the pawn early in the week, to get some cash to see her through until the Saturday pay day for my Da. The routine on a Saturday for me, as the youngest, was at my Maw's side after my Da got home from work and squared up the money, up to my Auntie Annie's in Camden Street, and then off we would go to Cumberland Street to the pawn to collect and pay for my Da's suit. The pawn was up a close on the first landing, and I remember a line of wooden doors leading into small booths. People would stand in an orderly queue on the landing, and wait their turn, and when a slot became available I would go in with my Maw. I remember guys wearing brown warehouse coats and shelves with stuff on them. The pawn ticket and money would be handed over by my Maw, and a couple of minutes later we had liberated my Da's togs for Saturday night.

We would come down from the pawn into Cumberland Street, which was one of the main shopping streets in the district, and then we were off to the butchers and fruit shop, and maybe even a treat like a wee malt loaf from Galbraith's store.

Around the corner from our house was a shop in Moffat Street, run by a big Irishman Neilly McFeely and his wife Mary. Neilly had a wee blue van which he loaded up every morning with all manner of stuff, and he would set off to the fledgling Castlemilk housing scheme, where he would blast his horn to let people know he was in the street and they could buy their groceries. The shop was left in the capable hands of Mary, a woman who enjoyed a flutter at the local bookies, and gave 'tick' to a limited few who she knew would pay at the end of the week. This was another source of credit which my wee Maw used to ensure we made it through another week.

Despite all the hardships, I wouldn't swap my Gorbals childhood for a King's ransom.

Tina Shields-Kerr

Maybe it was luck, maybe fortune, or even outright fate, whichever it was; life certainly threw a darn good chocolate covered pretzel my way the day we moved from Partick to the Gorbals. I came to know the Gorbals people as the salt of the earth, covered in chocolate, just like a chocolate pretzel. We landed in the Gorbals late 70's and sadly moved again, in 1986, back to Partick. The most formative years of my life were influenced entirely by my Gorbals experience.

Living in the tenements along the River Clyde all the kids in the street were dubbed "The Waterside Rats". I remember arriving in the Gorbals that first day and thinking how modern and new everything looked. My brother and I went out to play and immediately made friends with the kids in the street; friends that are still in my life today. We would be out from dawn til way past dusk. We settled very quickly into the local school, 'Wee Bonnies,' (St Bonaventure's Primary School) and then went onto John Bosco (a local secondary school). As the years progressed my brother and I joined in nicely with all the shenanigans and games going on in the Gorbals streets; chap the door runaway, helping the drunk men come home from "The Pig and Whistle" (protecting their nose from the fall), kick the can, five stones, sneaking into the gravie at night to see who was the bravest, oh and stealing a bar of Dairy Milk from R.S. McColl's (don't tell). The shenanigans got a little more questionable as we grew older. Some of our friends took a different road and slid into the world of heroin, glue sniffing, burglary and more. This point, as teenagers, was the major crossroads in a Gorbals life. "To do or not to do?" that was the question. The "to do" list for me was the cider in the ginger bottle and throwing up all night, going on a joy ride in a car that certainly wasn't mine, a few other little bad choices as a one-time deal, then realised I couldn't do 'that', 'that' would not be good....enough said! That was a far as my guts would take me!

Many little stories ensued along the way. One day I was in my hallway and I see a bag of white powder come through my letterbox, next minute five boys from the street come running through the close with the police at their backs. I remember just freezing on the spot and praying the door wouldn't chap. Gladly it didn't and the boys came back and asked for their goods. My wee ma was furious shouting at them all. Apologies were flying to the angry Mrs Shields, as they stood out of swinging reach and the day went on. Another occasion we had a cardboard cut-out on our broken window, and in the middle of the night we heard it getting cut open and one of the boys, we knew, was trying to break in to our house. This was to sadly assist with his new drug habit. The very next day my ma is coming back from the shops and the same boy helps her to the door with all her shopping. That was the day I saw the struggle these boys were going through. You see, the Gorbals had a way of letting you see into the rawness and desperateness of life as a junkie. These boys were good, but fell into a struggle with circumstance, peer pressure and willpower; salt and sweet, just like the chocolate pretzel.

Moving on as an adult who has emigrated to the USA, I bring with me a deep understanding and appreciation for a little place in Glasgow that showed me the heart of a community filled with humans who taught me about happiness, despair, humour, and outright grit. The experience has penetrated my head and heart to the core, and I thank the Lord above for such an opportunity in life. I have yet to live in another place that has filled my soul with such experience!

Everett Campbell Wylie

I was born and bred in the Gorbals, at 58 Eglinton Street. There were ten of us Wylie's.

I remember having to go to the steamie after school to help my ma with all the washing, a giant pram full of it. She would send me and my sister upstairs to the baths, (as there were very few, if any, houses in the Gorbals that had a bath in the house, people were sent to the "public baths" where housed a swimming pool as well as bath tubs) and we had to share the same bath and that was our weekly bath.

I used to love hanging oot the window with mum chatting, we lived one up in our tenement, especially the day all the taxies came along our street from town, it was magical.

Mum's sisters would send us wee dresses from Kearney, New Jersey, USA so my sister and I would go to the subway and do a full circle sitting quietly just so everyone would see our new dresses lol. (In Glasgow the subway does one complete run around the city, therefore you can join at Bridge Street station in the Gorbals and sit on the underground until it goes "full circle" and get off again when it comes back again). We would sit there aw proud because we had new clothes on.......oh how we appreciated the simple wee things, truly wonderful.

Pauline Sim

I was brought up in Sandyfaulds Street, Gorbals, Glasgow. The thing I remember most from that time was that all my family lived close by. My aunts, uncles and cousins all lived in the area in streets next to ours. Their doors were always open and I always had somewhere to go and cousins to play with. We all attended the same school, St Francis. There was a great community feeling and I always felt safe.

When I was eight we got a brand new house in Braehead Street, Oatlands, Glasgow. Most of our family were then scattered all over Glasgow and because my cousins now attended different schools, I only saw them and my aunts and uncles on a Saturday. I really missed them.

Most of the people who lived in the (then) new houses came from the Gorbals and brought with them the same community spirit that we had there. The children all played together and the adults looked after us. We use to play hide and seek in the graveyard, the Southern Necropolis even though we were told not to.

We still went to the Gorbals to shop, visit the library and go to chapel. My favourite place was Richmond Park. A great place to go and play, have picnics and feed the swans. The flower beds were always beautiful and well looked after. From our house in Braehead Street we used to walk through the park and over to the Barras on a Saturday to look for bargains and get a bag of whelks. At the Glasgow Fair we would walk over the bridge to the Glasgow Green when the shows were there to go on The Merry Go Round, the Dodgems, the Waltzers and the Motorbike rides and if you had any money left a bag of chips or candy floss on the way home.

Happy days.

John Hogan

I was born in Snowdon Street, Gorbals, Glasgow and moved to live in 24 St Enoch Square when I was 5 years old. My dad got the job as caretaker at the office block and the National Commercial Bank. I attended Gorbals Primary School at Buchan Street until I was 11 years old in 1964, going over the suspension bridge every day. I have many good memories of the Gorbals and my time at Buchan Street.

One story I would like to share with you is the time I and three pals skipped school at the afternoon break and went off on an adventure down the river. Remember the wee ferries that criss-crossed the Clyde? Well we had a great time going up and down the river from the Broomielaw to Govan and back again, daring each other to walk round the little ledge that ran around the side of the ferry or seeing who would go the furthest down the steps at the ferry landing stage. If you recall the river was always being dredged in those days and the sludge kept in big wooden vats at the side of the river until taken away. It was a hot summer day and the sludge looked very solid when it dried out. We had a discussion about whether or not it was solid enough to stand on, only one way to find out, yes, give it a go. My pal got in over the side and immediately sunk up to his waist in sludge. It stank and he had to walk home covered in the stuff.

He got absolutely battered when he got home. We all got taken in front of the Headmistress next day, I think her name was Mrs Smith or McKnight and received 5 of the belt each for skipping school. We also got it off our parents as well.

I tell you what though, it was well worth it. We had a great day and solved the question of the solidity of dredged sludge. I have so many great memories of my childhood in the Gorbals and although I moved away in 1964, I will always consider myself as coming from the Gorbals and do so with pride.

Helen Callanan McGarvie

I lived at 341 Caledonia Road, Gorbals, Glasgow and when my sister Mary and I got our first wage packet from work we decided to buy a present for our mother.

We took a walk over to the "Barras" over in the Gallowgate in the Calton area of Glasgow where there were barras/stalls with all sorts of people selling their different wares. We walked round and round looking at all the different stalls until we came to one run by a man calling himself "Glesga Harry." "Glesga Harry" was selling Pyrex tea sets, consisting of cups saucers etc and all the contents would be in a cardboard box and he was shouting out how these were "unbelievable" and how they were "unbreakable." To prove this point he would jump on top of one of the boxes with the tea sets in it then pick it up and throw it on the ground to prove that the contents were unbreakable saying "You'll have these for years."

So my sister Mary bought one of these tea sets and took it home and gave it to our mother who was over the moon with pleasure but saying how we should have bought something for ourselves instead of her.

Mary then called everyone into the kitchen to prove that this tea set was unbreakable and with everyone watching she picked up one of the cups from the box and threw in on the kitchen floor where it immediately broke into a thousand pieces. Our mother had never had a tea set before so Mary went back over to the Barras and stood beside this "Glesga Harry's" stall and telling all the potential customers don't buy anything from him as he's a conman. Harry was losing so much custom that he gave Mary another tea set just to get rid of her, so our Mother got a brand new tea set once again.

So all was well that ended well.

Years ago when we lived in our tenement my pal Irene and I were going to the roller skating but my mum said that I had to wash the stairs before I went out.

My mum was going to the local pub to get a carry out for herself and her sisters. As she was leaving she put on my coat (previously my pal Irene had been wearing it and had left her fags in one of the pockets) and my mum went mad and wouldn't believe that the cigarettes didn't belong to me.

Well she gave me a battering, and then she went and kicked the pail with the dirty water in it down all the stairs and made me wash them all over again. I still don't smoke to this day and haven't seen my pal Irene again, ah well I lived to tell the story, oh and I got to go to the roller skating the following night.

Cath Dorran (née Gibb)

I was born in 400b Moffat Street, Gorbals, Glasgow in my granny's house. The year was 1954 and it was very common for a mother to deliver her baby at home; sometimes with the help of a midwife, sometimes just the woman next door who had hopefully done it before.

Our house was 21 Errol Street, Gorbals, Glasgow. This was a small street behind Cumberland Street and off Camden Street. I lived there with my ma and da and eleven months later my sister Trisha was born, followed five years later by my sister Marie. My ma, (Mary Anne Bridget Gibb née Brolly) had been ill with Trisha, so she had been delivered in the Rottenrow Hospital in the "toon". When it came to the birth of Marie, she suffered even more and had to go into St Francis Nursing Home. Marie was baptised at birth because they were worried she wouldn't survive. I'm forever grateful that she battled through the night and today, the only evidence of that traumatic night is a slight hearing deficit.

The house we shared was a room and kitchen which was typical for most families in the Gorbals. There was a bed recess in the living room where my parents slept and we three shared the single remaining room. The toilet was outside in the back close as most were in those days. We shared with our toilet with 3 other families. I never knew the luxury of an inside toilet until I was almost 15 and we moved to the maisonettes on Old Rutherglen Road.

Across the street from us was the "Hibs Hall". Many a Saturday night I lay awake listening to the sound of music and laughter spilling from the building. Next door to us was the "League of the Cross Hall", then further on "St Francis Boys Club." This was also the home of the St Francis Pipe Band. It was a lively wee street to say the least and our house was no stranger to a party either!

My ma was the only girl with eight brothers so when my granny died in 1959, 21 Errol Street became the focal point for my ma's family and there was never a shortage of company! My paternal grandparents lived up the same close as us but they were almost tee totals and very reserved in comparison to the Brolly's. My ma had a cracking sense of humour and was always full of nonsense and fun. I'll never forget when she made her brother a piece (sandwich) with a jam lid in the middle; he nearly broke his false teeth when he took a bite! My da (Jimmy), on the other hand, was the quiet man in comparison. He didn't go to the pub, but he did love the bookies. Shawfield on a Friday night was his pleasure.

My sisters and I went to St Francis Primary School. I loved that school. We also went to 12 o'clock Mass on a Sunday in St Francis Chapel. Trisha, my pal and me sold the papers at the back of the chapel, 'The Observer' and 'The Universe.' One Sunday, Trisha brought a 'pal'. To my horror, she revealed her pet white mouse from her top pocket. The mouse, of course, decided it was time for a great escape and darted off down the middle aisle whilst the Priest was saying Mass. What a laugh!

As much as I loved my primary school I loved the summer holidays too. The days always seemed to be sunny giving us the opportunity to play in the street all day until dark, only going in for dinner. The older girls in our street would put on a "Variety Show" in the middle of the road - there was no traffic so we had the run of the place. The show usually began with the 'Tiller Girls' performing their cabaret act, then they would all take turns of singing which kept us amused for hours!

During one of these long balmy days, a wee girl from the end close joined us. It seemed to me that her ma was always having babies. In my ma's words "She was a poor soul who did nae have much." (Weren't we all?!)

My Ma took pity on her and brought the wee girl into our house. She washed her up at the sink and changed her into my sister Marie's clothes before sending her back out to play with a piece n' jam. The wee girl's ma was delighted. I always think this story typifies the spirit of the Gorbals - everyone looked out for all us kids. Mind you, they checked us as well, it wasn't uncommon for the woman in number 11 to come out and give us all what for.

When I was 16, I finished my schooling at Holyrood Secondary School and met my husband Ronnie, and got married in St Bonaventure's. We moved further south and lived in Simshill, although for the past two years we've been living in Sydney. We came here to join our three children Jamie, Lisa and Gary.

Today the name "Gorbals" is synonymous with violence and deprivation. Yes, we were poor but so was everyone, but I was never witness to the violence and I never felt unsafe. The Gorbals was a great community, people looked out for each other and that's a rare thing these days. There were many people in the Gorbals with a "heart of gold" - they would literally give you their last penny.

Many children of the Gorbals have achieved great things in life across a variety of disciplines like sport, art, literature, music and commerce. This is a testament to the spirit of the Gorbals that shaped our young lives and gave us resilience and character.

I am very proud to say I was born and raised in the Gorbals.

Brian Donnelly

I was born and stayed in Oatlands, Glasgow.

Through the 1950's and 60's I stayed in the old part of the area which was run down, was unsanitary and had overcrowded housing. I have never regretted one moment of my life in the area.

As a child I had many friends who were from similar backgrounds, we all mixed and spent our free time outside, playing in all kinds of weather conditions, all kinds of games that were handed down from our parents. We were blessed with having a wonderful public park across the road which gave us endless opportunities to play. We were able to take a ball across the Kay Bridge (please see below) and play at football for hours. We may not have appreciated it at the time but we had schools staffed with excellent teachers whose dedication was to equip us for the future.

Due to most people in the area living similar lifestyles, materialism did not exist in our lives and everyone seemed to accept each other as equals and as children we learned to respect older people.

I have managed to live my life as a hard working individual with good old fashioned values, and I now look back on it and put some of my success down to being lucky enough to have been brought up in Oatlands.

Kay Bridge

The Kay Bridge was also known as Polmadie Bridge and is approximately in the middle of Richmond Park (please see photo in the book). The bridge leads from the end of Polmadie Road/Rutherglen Road and crosses over to where the football pitches in Glasgow Green are, also known as "Flesher's Haugh." I think Mr Kay was involved on the political scene in Glasgow and the bridge was named after him in his honour. So, if you can imagine, the Kay Bridge is almost in the middle of between Kings Bridge heading to Bridgeton Cross and Rutherglen Bridge at Shawfield Stadium.

David Scott

I was born at 341 Caledonia Road in the Gorbals area in 1967. There were four blocks of flats altogether, these being 305 Caledonia Road, 341 Caledonia Road, 487 Cumberland Street and 474 Old Rutherglen Road. Sadly only 341 Caledonia Road and 305 Caledonia Road now remain. There have also been a lot of changes to the area with new housing, shops and new roads. The area around the flats was redesigned after the demolition of 487 Cumberland Street and 474 Old Rutherglen Road. The rubble from these flats was used to fill in the area where the tunnels and monkey bars/puzzle once stood.

What sticks in my memory most is playing cops and robbers under 341 block where the garages once were, and riding my budgie bike down the ramp at 341 and coming out at the monkey puzzle just where the Phoenix bar stood.

I also remember as a child coming back from town on a Saturday afternoon and sitting on the big concrete seat outside the Phoenix bar with a can of juice and a bag of crisps while my mum went into the Phoenix lounge to see my dad.

I also remember going into Joe's paper shop and the Spar shop next door then Taylor's dentist was next to the Spar. I also used to enjoy going down the ramp at the Phoenix on my plastic yellow skateboard while receiving a few cuts and bruises, (of course).

Another thing that sticks in my memory was doing a "workie" on the swings and standing on the swing to make it go higher. Unfortunately, I tried to do this without using my hands and I went over the bar of the swing and landed on the black fence breaking both of my wrists (being a kid I thought I was brave enough).

I also remember the ambulance at the time, a dark blue coloured one (Does anyone else remember these ambulances?), this may be around 1973 onwards.

I had a happy childhood growing up in the Gorbals and I'm still living here in the Gorbals today.

Memories right enough.

Margaret Fullerton

This is a wee story for you about the pawn shop which our parents and grandparents used to all use, (well a good many of them did), years ago in the Gorbals and Oatlands area.

When my dad, John Kavanagh, who lived in Florence Street was much younger his mother, Daisy Kavanagh told him to go across the road to The Tavern (pub) with my Grandad Paddy's painting overalls as he had been to a funeral earlier on in the day and was wearing his suit. She said to my dad to tell his da to go into the toilet in the pub, take off his suit and put his overalls on and pretend he was going to work, so that she could take his suit to the pawn shop. This was so she would get some money at the pawn for the suit to help buy some food for the weekend to feed all the family.

Yes, the Gorbals has changed over the years and a lot of people moved away to all those new housing schemes after the Gorbals clearance, but my own mum, also called Margaret (nee Docherty) still stays in the Gorbals in Hallside Place across from the police station in Cumberland Street.

That's my wee story about the pawn shop and how it helped us out in our hours of need.

Ann Ward (nee Clark)

I was born n bred in Hospital Street, Gorbals, Glasgow in 1959 and lived there until 1973. My favourite pastime whilst waiting on my wee da finishing his pint in the Clelland Bar, was skating up and doon outside the bar. It was a great street for skating on. My old skate would have been tied up with my ma's good American Tan nylons (tights).

After a while my oot came ma da and he would say "Take yer ma's wages up and tell her I'm having another pint, I won't be long!!!!" Off I went and to my delight my ma allowed me to go back oot on ma own with my skate!!

Being the eldest of 8 this was a treat not having to look after the others, so off I skated back doon to the Clelland with its big, wide smooth road, skating until my skate started to come apart in the middle!!!! I tried to put it back together tying ma ma's nylons tighter n tighter but no, it just kept coming away. Heartbroken, I went into the bar to tell ma da who had now moved to the lounge watching the go-go dancers!!! My da told me to go round the corner, opposite the wee swings and ask the man in the garage to put "nut n bolt" in!!! So off I went and asked the man for his help. "Nae bother hen, give me it here!" and in no time ma skate was sorted!!! I was delighted and thanked the man. Funny thing was I never ever got a "pair o skates" just thought I was so lucky way the one!!!!! I played with it for hours and reluctantly, let my wee sister Helen have a shot, but kept it planked fae my brothers Jim and John in case they broke it!!!!

Telling this story to ma weans they just can't believe how poor we were and happy just the same.

Anne Marie Millar (nee McAuley)

I started life at 270 Cumberland Street, Gorbals, Glasgow and then moved to House 20D, 305 Caledonia Road also in the Gorbals when the flats first opened. I remember the smell of the freshness the first time we went to see the house. My brother Pat and I both thought it was huge, yet it only had 2 bedrooms.

I remember I was around 16 or 17 years of age, I was looking after my disabled father, Pat, after losing my mother, Jeanie at 16.

It was a scorcher of a summer, and not being able to go on holidays due to circumstances, my sun trap was the hill in the "gravie." Me and my friends would go over and place our blankets on the ground and sunbathe, but that year I got more than a sun tan.

When I went home I knew I had a burn so the "Calamine Lotion" came out, but it was much worse than just "a burn," I had to have the doctor make a house call as I'd started to become delirious, and at one point I couldn't move my arms, so panic sets in and worsens things. I remember the doctor giving me a brown paper bag to blow into. I never went over to the "gravie" again to sunbathe, I'd learnt my lesson.

While at the "gravie" we were always respectful while there and took our juice bottles and sweetie papers with us when we left. The section we sunbathed at was turning right at the centre, going into that section and heading towards Cally (Caledonia) Road.

These really were good auld days and I wouldn't change them.

Lynne Lees

I guess you could say I'm Gorbals through and through, three out of four of my grandparents were immigrants.

My paternal grandmother was called Elsie Doherty and was Southern Irish, or 'black' Irish on account of her dark hair and colouring.

My mother's father, Cornelius O'Connell came to the Gorbals as a very young man, rumoured to be sent over from Ireland for "The Smashing of the van" (the incident involving an IRA prisoner that happened on the High Street as he was being transported from St Andrew's Square police court cells to Duke Street Prison).

My mother's mother, Nellie Savoakas was born in Govan Street (now Ballater Street) to Josef Savoakas a miner from Lithuania and Nan Zylesky a young Lithuanian girl. I'm not sure they were married as Josef was never spoke about, and the family history, as I remember it, was that Nan and Nellie were raised as sisters, being Roman Catholics it was all very hush hush.

In the early half of the 20th Century, there was much prejudice against immigrants and many had to change their names in order to gain employment, so Nellie Savoakas became Helen Lees (which is a coincidence as my mother later married a certain James Lees) she married Cornelius O'Connell of Sandyfaulds Street in Saint Francis Roman Catholic Church in 1929. They settled into a tenement in Naburn Street and had three children, Cornelius, Thomas and Catherina. Sadly Cornelius contracted TB and he died aged only 18 months.

My mother, Catherina (Catherine or Rena) was born in 1935. Sadly my grandparents' marriage disintegrated and my mother and her brother Tommy never saw their father again after he left the family home when my mother was very young, about 7 years old. She never forgot him though, and often sang the Irish folk song 'Kevin

Barry' to me as she fondly remembered her father singing it to her as a child.

My grandmother often worked long hours and she also loved socialising. My great granny (Nan) moved briefly to Maryhill and took my Uncle Tommy there, so my ma would spend a lot of time looking after herself and often she would spend time in one of the many Gorbals cinemas of the 1940's and 1950's and she developed a love of cinema and music which she passed on to me, I'm glad to say! My mother attended Saint Bonaventure's Primary School, then passed the test for Holyrood 'Senior Secondary' which she didn't like so went to 'Big Bonnies' instead.

She left school and took employment as a sales assistant in the record/music department in Lewis's Department Store in Argyle Street, Glasgow. She loved the job and often recounted to me the time she met the Andrews Sisters when she worked there and she was very proud of that, such a happy memory for her. She enjoyed fashion too, and would save all her wages for the latest fashions of the day.

When she left Lewis's she worked as a machinist in Sylbraides in Commerce Street, then as a clippie 'oan the buses' where she met my dad, Jimmy Lees, who was a bus driver from Gloucester Street in Tradeston. They married very young, my ma was only 18 and on the 30th October 1953 they had a double wedding in St Francis Roman Catholic Church as my Uncle Tommy married his wife the very same day! Sadly neither marriage survived, though my parents had two daughters, my sister Laraine Lees (born 1956) and me.

My father unfortunately developed a chronic alcohol problem. He was a very handsome man with thick jet black hair and very smartly dressed, but sadly that all deteriorated when drink took over, and he ended up in and out of prison, which sadly is where he was when I was born in September 1963. My ma had already decided enough was enough and ended the marriage.

My father never recovered from alcoholism and died in the early 1980s in his 50s. I had only met him a handful of times but can still remember him meeting us when he was living in a homeless hostel and we were waiting on a bus in town to go to Calderpark Zoo for the day. I was very young, about four, but even then it was sad.

The main man in my life when I was very young was my Granny Nellie's second husband, Peter Taylor, a great old Glasgow character (although he was born in Wishaw!) who worked in the Co-operative building in McNeil Street , which was like a fairytale castle to me as a child. Peter was the manager in the 'board wash' department, the workers all loved him as he used to start his shift every morning with a fly 'slug' of his favourite tipple, Eldorado, and that would set him up for the day!

My Ma found things hard, she was a single mother to me and my sister Laraine and we lived in a two room tenement in McNeil Street, the close next to the Pig and Whistle. Now and again my dad would turn drunk up singing "Please release me, let me go' (the Engelbert Humperdink hit) outside the door, but he would get chased pronto!!

In 1967 we moved to 474 Old Rutherglen Road, House 18D, which were nice flats and we had great neighbours. My granny by that time had been moved out to Cranhill from the Gorbals and in fact I was baptised there in Saint Maria Goretti's Church on Bellrock Street in October 1963.

My granny would come down on the bus from Cranhill to babysit us when my ma got a job in a pub in Kinning Park where she met my stepdad, John McLean. He was a great man, kind and gentle. He worked in the Merchant Navy and they got married in June 1968. My brother, John, was born in our house on the 18th floor on 3rd March 1970. The radio was on and the song playing was Lee Marvin singing "Wandering star." Very apt song for the son of a merchant seaman I think!

One of my happiest memories of growing up in the Gorbals in the seventies was the John Mains Community Centre Disco on a Friday night, affectionately known as "Sooty's Disco." We would only have been about ten or eleven years old but it was the highlight of the week for us.

David Andrews was the DJ, playing all the latest hits from the pop music charts, I remember the songs 'Kung Fu Fighting' by Carl Douglas, 'The Black Superman' by Mohammed Ali and all the songs by the Bay City Rollers, I remember those best as they had special dances we would all enthusiastically shuffle round the dance floor to in our platform shoes doing all the moves.........!

At the end of the night there would be a "Moonie," (a slow dance) usually a Donny Osmond or David Cassidy number and everyone would shuffle around with their partner looking uncomfortable and holding them at arm's length.

The John Mains Community Centre also held talent competitions and some of the acts were very good. I remember Annette Welsh and Jan Smith had a really cool majorette routine twirling and dancing to "Bye Bye Baby" sang by the Bay City Rollers. I still remember wishing I was doing something like that, but our school (Hayfield Primary) had our class doing a horrible tune on our Recorders, we were probably last in the competition every year ha ha.

I was lucky enough to be a teenager in the 70's! Such exciting fashions and music, as young girls we followed all the latest crazes. I was 14 years old when DISCO came into fashion, the styles and music were amazing, glitter, glamour and brilliant music to dance to, it was really exciting and such an wonderful time. I always remember the sun shining when I was a teenager , don't remember the rainy days at all!

The most exciting memory I have from that era was the release of SATURDAY NIGHT FEVER, one of the biggest movies of 1977 (along with STAR WARS and CLOSE ENCOUNTERS, it really was a great year for cinema goers). I watched Barry Norman's show about the latest releases in the movies and fell immediately loved John Travolta and his amazing dance moves.

The chart hits of the summer were all from that movie, 'Night Fever', 'How deep is your Love' and 'Staying alive'. I just knew I had to see the movie, and all my friends had the same idea. Saturday night

Fever was showing at our local, The Coliseum, we just had to get in there undetected as it was an X rating or a AA (can't remember which) so that meant you had to be 18 years old. We came up with a plan! We worked out who kinda looked oldest in our gang, somehow Mick Price drew the short straw haha! He had to pay in at the door, then go and kick open the fire exit to let the rest of us in, myself, Caroline Hughes, Anne Lithgow, Lorraine McGeorge, Sharon Morton, the McMillan twins, Marie Gallagher, Alan Sinclair, Davie McKay and Brian McCann all waited anxiously at the back door....BANG!!! The door flew open!!! We were in!!! We ran up the stairs anxiously and trying to stifle our excited laughter, we found our way past 'auld John' the Irish concierge who normally had eyes like a hawk and somehow before we knew it we were sitting down watching the adverts before the big movie! Woohoo! We were so excited, and when the movie started rolling and 'Staying Alive' was booming out as John Travolta swaggered down that Brooklyn Street in the opening scene, we were all on cloud nine!

The film was absolutely amazing and the atmosphere and music of the film was perfect for Gorbals teenagers who could really relate to the characters on screen who escaped the boredom of everyday life with fashion and music. I can honestly say that was the best movie experience I ever had and I've carried it with me all my life, my friends all remember it too.

It was a sad day when the Coliseum shut down as it was the last and probably the grandest of the Gorbals cinemas and I'm sure many people like me had very happy memories of that wonderful place.

The Gorbals sometimes poor in pocket, always rich in character, sometimes sad in story, always filled with hope. Sometimes homes were crumbling, always homes were welcoming, sometimes hearts were weary, always hearts were loving, the Gorbals always my home.

That's a brief history of my family and my life in the Gorbals; the Gorbals had many wonderful stories, every one different, every one special, every one important, and thanks for reading mine.

May Sweeney

I was born in Thistle Street, Gorbals, Glasgow in 1952 and was christened in St Francis' Church in Cumberland Street. I moved to Oatlands, Glasgow when I was one year and we stayed in Cramond Street and along with my ma and da there were 6 of us, Billy, Geana, myself, Barbara, Martin and Thomas. We had a brilliant upbringing and we were a close and loving family doing everything together from going to Richmond Park and The Ritz Picture House, where we got free passes for as my ma worked there.

We played in the streets at peever, beds, and of course balls and ropes. We used to play in the backs at wee houses, with our dolls and prams, also shops, and now and again we put wee concerts on.

Another wee bit of information is when I was about 10 years old we moved to Croftfoot Crescent, Castlemilk, Glasgow and I attended St Bartholomew's Primary School. We were there for about a year and my ma hated it with not being able to settle down as she had been born and raised in the soo-side and missed it so much and it broke her heart every day. My da at that time went to work down south in England as that was where big money was in those days. My ma ended up giving up her four apartment house in Castlemilk and took us all back to a room and kitchen in Crammond Street in the Oatlands again which ma and da bought with money saved from my da's wage earnings in England, and hey ho, we were all happy again back in oor wee room and kitchen in the soo-side.

When I was teenager we moved to Polmadie Road. It was fantastic to get a 2 room and kitchen with bathroom, that was a luxury.

I used to hang about Mario's Fish and Chip Shop in Polmadie Road, that's where everybody met, but my ma didn't like me doing that because we were a bit rowdy, but in those days it was all good clean fun. So if any of the gang spotted my ma or da they warn me and I would duck down and hide.

When I was 15 I started work. I was so lucky as my first job was in the Gorbals Co-op Offices in Coburg Street.

Another wee thing about my teenage years is that I used to help Father Cunningham (a Priest in St Bonaventure's Catholic Church on Caledonia Road) to run Wee Bonnie's disco and many a good night we had there, and a few lumbers lol.

After that I married and yes, guess what, my first house was back in Cramond Street, so that was me back to my roots. I had 3 lovely children there Barbara, Paula and Derek, and then in 1974 we were told we had to leave as building was getting renovated. It was a sad day leaving my beloved Oatlands behind, it broke my heart as I had so many lovely childhood friends and the best neighbours anyone could ask for, too many to mention, even today my memory still goes back there as it was where I spent my school days in Wee Bonnie's and Big Bonnie's.

I also had 6 wonderful years in 170 Sandiefield Road in the Gorbals. When I moved to Sandiefield Road I met a lot of new friends who among them were Cathy and Irene. We were very close and we called ourselves "Charlie's Angels." I was Farrah Fawcett Majors as I had the same hair style.

We had many a good night in the "Granite City Pub" and also the "Railway Club." We never missed a ladies night when all the neighbours got together, they were rare old nights.

Now the reason why I left Sandiefield Road was the breakup of my marriage if it wasn't for that I would never have left the Gorbals.

Patricia Docherty

I would like to tell you a wee story about my late grandmother Mary, who lived in the maisonettes in Hutchensontown Court in the Gorbals. She was a regular customer at the Phoenix Public House nearby. They called her Mary "the boomerang" because when she was worse for wear due to the whisky, a member of the bar staff would take her home, make sure she was safe in her house, then lock her door and post her keys through the letterbox. Within fifteen minutes she "escaped" and was once more back in the pub hence the nickname "Boomerang Mary".

One story about one of my granny's "escapes" actually happened when I was on my first date with my now husband, David. It was a summer's night about 9.30 pm and myself and David were sitting on a wall of a grass verge outside of my granny's kitchen window and our first date was almost over.

My granny's kitchen window opened very slowly, a handbag was thrown out of the window, and two feet appeared, followed by legs. It was my granny "escaping" back to the Phoenix Pub. Margaret McGuigan Bonner who worked in the Phoenix had taken her home, locked the door and posted the door keys through the letterbox as was the normal.

My granny was that drunk she couldn't find the keys and this was why she was "escaping" from her house via the kitchen window. Well David shouted out "Oh my God, look at that wee wummin dreeping out of that window." Luckily enough she lived on the ground floor but the window was quite high. I couldn't move for laughing, I didn't know whether to laugh or greet, so I turned round to David and said "Now you've met my granny, do you still want to go out with me?"

This was just one of the stories in regards to my granny "Boomerang Mary" and her trips to the Phoenix Public House.

John Noble

I was born in the tenements of those lovely buildings all along Roseberry Street in Oatlands, Glasgow, my mum and dad being Ina and Donnie Noble.

There was so much to do and play at when we were kids, and we were always going over to Richmond Park which was just only a stone's throw away on Rutherglen Road. There was the rockery and swing park where we used to all love going to when we were kids and I always remember sliding down that great chute oh and the monkey bars, we would swing one arm in front of the other trying to get from one end to the other.

Talking about the swings, we used to go to "Jenny's Burn" which ran through Richmond Park, and there was always a rope tied to one of the trees and we all liked to think we were Tarzan as we swung over "Jenny's Burn," although once or twice one of us would slip off of the rope and fall into the burn. The burn had a terrible smell coming from it, because some chemical firms on the industrial estate opposite Shawfield Stadium used to off load their waste into it, giving "Jenny's Burn" a smell that would bring tears to your eyes.

There was such a great community spirit in those days in Oatlands and all the neighbours seemed to know each other and they always kept their eyes on us kids as we played in the streets. There was a leisure centre there that produced so many fine football players and it was run by a man called Mr Brian Adams. I had the honour of playing for Clyde FC (nicknamed "The Bully Wee") and they were a great wee football team playing all their home matches in Shawfield Stadium before they moved from there to Cumbernauld.

I have so many happy memories of Oatlands, and all the great people and friends who lived there, and I'm just happy to leave a few of my memories here in my wee story.

Isabel Horan

I was born in Alice Street in Oatlands and went to Wolseley Street School which was only a few minutes' walk away from our single end. We had St Bonaventure's Chapel and St Margaret's Church and two schools, St Bonaventure's (Primary and Junior Secondary] and Wolseley Street Primary.

My first memories are of always playing in the back courts and streets and getting tar on my sand shoes [sannies] in the hot summer months when the tarmacadam melted on the pavements. Little did we know when playing wee shops with a brick as the shop counter and raking midgies for goods to sell that we were learning our first social skills.

Then all the neighbours who were doing their windae hingin would watch over us as as were taking turns of playing skipping ropes or playing kick the can or maybe a game of peever. The rag and bone man would come round and we get old claes from our ma's which we gladly gave to him in exchange for a balloon or maybe a whistle if you were lucky.

Richmond Park was our own very own paradise, the sand pit [sonny pon] the swings and not forgetting the ducksie. We would play there for hours until we were hungry, or perhaps we had taken a piece with margarine dipped in sugar (healthy?), a milk bottle with water in it and a liquorice stick dipped into it to make the water become Ginger lol ah pure bliss.

We had Rutherglen Road, our very own Argyle Street with chemists, the cafes, Tunnock's sweetie shop, bookies, pubs, post office, a funeral parlour and fish and chip shops etc and then we had Frank and Angelina's newsagents shop beside the Glue Pot Pub in Wolseley Street and you could buy almost anything in there, except clothes, and how I loved their shop window at Christmas, it was really magical.

I moved out to Castlemilk in 1956/1957 but my granny still stayed there in Alice Street and I went back to live there with her, and we sadly watched the demolition of the soo-side when they started to tear down our dear Oatlands bit by bit. We owe so much to our parents and grandparents for bringing us up in that small but beautiful place called Oatlands; it was our own wee paradise.

Even though I now live in Cumbernauld my memories still go back to that magic time and place.

James Hart

On the 16 November 1950 yours truly appeared to an expectant crowd gathered outside the delivery room in Rottenrow Maternity Glasgow. I weighed in at a healthy 8lbs 14ozs, the eldest son of Tommy and Ella Hart.

In those days it was a 7 day stay in hospital before you went home. Home for me would be the Gorbals at 79 Naburn Street, the place that I would take my first tentative steps in the world. As we all knew, albeit maybe at a later stage, life would be the making, or breaking, of so many souls from our little piece of territory within the sprawling city that was home to over 1.2M people, Glasgow.

Everything went well for the next 2 ½ years then my sister arrived and to my way of thinking somehow stole my thunder. I was now the big brother and I was now expected to look after my sister. So at the tender age of 3, I became a bouncer to patrol her pram, and keep as much as a fly from going near her. Things started move along and in late 1953 the family was the talk of the steamie!!!! We were off to America, to be precise Gastonia, North Carolina. My mother, who herself had only been in Glasgow for 6 years after travelling from Vienna in Austria, in 1947 after the war where she had met and married my dad Tommy or 'Toorie' as he was known by his mates.

The big adventure started with us leaving Glasgow by train to Southampton where we boarded the Queen Mary to sail us to New York. We arrived in New York after a 7 day voyage across the Atlantic Ocean, being met on arrival by my aunt, my mother's sister, who herself being a war bride, had married a yank and travelled from Vienna after the war had ended, and was happily settled in Gastonia, where we were to live, it turns out for only 1 year.

The 2nd year we move to Cherryville, that's where my dad was working. It was closer to his work than in Gastonia, but we were home again in Glasgow the following year, as mum just could not stand the heat at night during the long summers.

We arrived back in Glasgow just in time for me to begin school at St Francis Primary. I can even remember our Primary 1 teacher a Miss Moate. Miss Moate's claim to fame at that period in my short life was she would get chased by some of the boys, because she rode home on a scooter, and we would try to catch her as she headed home to the Shawlands area of town, which I happened to find out in years to come.

For the next 3 years it was a sharp learning curve as a boy growing up in the Gorbals. It was if you ran with the right crowd, it was your street against their street, you protected your piece of turf and for us it was the swing park in Hutchesontown Square/Naburn Street. Like all boys of our age the fights were all long distance battles shouting at each other 100 yards apart. Christ, when you think on it now, you could have had a game of football going on between the protagonists and never miss a kick of the ball.

We have now reached that afore mentioned date once again 16 November only this time it's 1958. Yes people, yours truly's 8th birthday, and apart from the family's 'Happy Birthday' wishes that was it. Busy, busy day that birthday turned out for that was the day we left the Gorbals for a brand new build in Castlemilk, the largest housing scheme in Europe at that time. We moved into our brand new home with bathroom and other things not to common in the Gorbals that we had just left. We started to settle in as Castlemilk expanded and the schools were built, so this meant that travelling back down to St Francis every day was no longer needed, as we had been getting picked up by bus every day and taken to our old schools. The schools, the shops, and the arcade were all built and within a few years we became a self sustaining area. The vast majority of the population of Castlemilk had come from the Gorbals, although dispersed all about the scheme. Life was good in the new house, brighter, cleaner, a better standard of life from the old ways of tin baths in front of an open fire, but that had its romance also, because until you've had a bath in front of an open fire you've never lived.

Now that brings me to the present day .... Just Another Saturday.

The alarm rings 7.30 am, it's not a school day so no time for hanging about in bed. I've got to be ready for just after 8.00 am, a lot to do today. I travel down to the Gorbals every Saturday morning, get to my maw's house (Granny's), 152 Cally (Caledonia) Road, I'm first up.

It's across the road to the Fruiterers but just for the durty veg, chap next door see if auld Annie needs anything while I'm there, get their veg and back up 3 flights of stairs. Drop of the dirty veg, then it's down to Cumberland Street to Rita's for the clean veg and any fruit that my maw needs. The Co-op next port of call for the Co-op's plain bread and milk was all she ever bought, and don't forget the 'Divvy.' Life would not have been worth living had I forgotten her dividend ticket. Back up those 3 lots of stairs again. The early shopping done meant my maw would start on the lunch for us all later that day. I would then have breakfast with my uncle John, he would then get washed and shaved, he'd go into his room and dress, when he was ready we walked up to Eglinton Street.

My uncle was a window cleaner and had a window round out in Pollok and every Saturday we both went out there to collect his 'window money' for that week. As an 11 year old, I did all the 2 ups and for my pains I was allowed to keep all my tips, which in those times amounted to a fair auld amount some weeks. Between my tips and all my pocket money I could maybe muster just over a pound for my Saturday's labours.

Back home in the Gorbals by this time it's nearly 1.00 pm. Just in time for lunch. My uncle James would be there when we get in, and he would ask me to nip down to Findley's the paper shop, which was on the corner of Cally Road and Naburn Street, across from Wee Pat Fagan's the bookies. I collect James' stuff and take it back up those 3 flights of stairs. God Rest him, on thinking of those times I realise that he just sent me on those errands just to justify giving me a half crown for my pocket money.

Those are the times that I remember with such sad fondness. Times before those in their infinite wisdom decided on decimating a part of the city that had a heart that was bigger than Glasgow itself, the place that I was born, and the place that I am proud to tell anyone who would ask. This is because it's people are the salt of the earth and they instilled in me a set of values that I have taught my family, and I hope they will do the same, because family values was what the Gorbals was all about, helping out family, friends and neighbours when needed, because, you never knew when it would be your turn.

I didn't know then that within a few short years, the Gorbals that we knew would be no more. The shops, the cinemas, the pubs were all demolished, and more importantly, the people scattered to all the four corners of Glasgow. Pollok and Castlemilk in the south, out to Drumchapel in the west, Easterhouse and Cranhill in the east and Barmulloch and Balornock in the north. Scattered to the four corners of the ever expanding city, with no, or very few familiar faces in these new and vastly sprawling estates.

However, like bad pennies we returned to what we called home. The 'Dampies', the high rises, Queen Elizabeth Square, and the rest of the new builds. Slowly but surely the people started to return, back to familiar streets, familiar faces, back to normality for them, back to an era now forever gone, but that will never be forgotten, instilled in hearts by their parents, their families and their friends. Memories and stories, some vastly garnished to enhance a reputation, stories of people that did extremely brave and courageous acts and deeds for friends, family and neighbours and totally shunned any form of acknowledgement for things they did and accomplished.

The New Gorbals, although the houses are a far cry from the old tenements the same sense of know your neighbour has never returned, which is sad. Those who moved back still carry on the old ways to try to install a code, an order which our grandparents and parents lived by. We look after our own in the Gorbals, that's the way of things, that's the way we do things, the Gorbals way.

Emily Biros

I was a 'Blitz Baby' born March 1941 at the Rottenrow Maternity Hospital in Glasgow. Mum told me that the city was being bombed that night, my dad a soldier was sent overseas shortly after I was born. We lived in Oatlands on Rutherglen Road between the Ritz Picture House and Waterside Street in a single end (one room) two stories up, our window faced the River Clyde and we could see the park, Glasgow Green across the water from our window.

With all the bombings that were going on, my mum was told we needed to evacuate. We were sent to a small village in the lead hills called Wanlochead where a family took us in and we stayed there for a few years. I can still remember being there even though I was very young at the time. When I was four years old my dad returned from the war and I can remember that day too. It was strange having him there as the only males I had been around was my grandfather and a few uncles.

A year later my sister was born and then I started school at Oatlands School and I had many new friends and I loved school. There were plenty of other kids to play with up the back court after school and we played games like peever, whip and peerie and hide and seek. I also learned to climb dykes which were really a bit on the dangerous side but being kids we had no fear. We did other things that were naughty like tying two doors handles together with a bit of rope or string (on the tenement stairhead landings) and bang on the doors and run away. At one time I got caught by a policeman and he gave me hell for doing this but let me go after giving me a warning.

As I got older I would go to the matinee at the Ritz Picture House or the Paragon Picture House on Cumberland Street. There were always good Cowboy and Indian films being shown. Another favourite of mine was going to Richmond Park with my pals where we would take a fishing net and an old milk bottle or jam jar and try and catch baggie minnies or tadpoles, and if we did we put our catch into them and we could spend the whole day doing that.

I went to the Church of Scotland on Pine Street every Sunday morning and in the afternoon I went to Sunday School at a Church on Cumberland Street. I joined the Brownies and was in the Church choir and took part in the Church plays. I took up tap dancing lessons but didn't stick with it. About this time my other sister was born. We spent a lot of time at my grandparents' house in Hospital Street, Gorbals and I loved going there as I also had friends who lived there too. The Gorbals had a bad reputation (wrongly) but we never saw any trouble there.

My mum was born and raised in Wolseley Street while my dad was raised across from the Southern Necropolis Graveyard on Caledonia Road. I loved Christmas and New Year time as we all went to my grandparents for parties where I would meet up with my aunts, uncles and cousins. There would be lots of food and lots of singing, especially just after the 'bells' rang in the new year. When I was ten years old we left Oatlands to live in the Calton (just up from Glasgow Cross) as it was a bigger house. It was so sad to leave the soo-side and my friends and my school but I got over it.

After my qualifying exams I went to St John's Senior Secondary school and during this time my brother was born. We then moved out to Castlemilk (a new housing scheme on the outskirts of Glasgow). It was always my dream to come to the States and I emigrated here in 1960. I married and have a daughter and now live in Southern California. I have never forgotten my homeland and I am a very proud Scot. With my upbringing it has made me the strong woman that I am today.

I would like to thank Danny Gill for writing this book and for letting me be a part of it, thanks for letting me share my story.

CHAPTER 3

Songs

Oor wee school's the best wee school, the best wee school in Glesga
The only thing that's wrang wae it, is the baldy heided Master,
He goes tae the pub on a Saturday night, he goes tae the Church on Sunday
He prays to God to give him strength, tae belt the weans on Monday.

Wan two three o'Leary
I saw Wallace Beary
kissing Shirley Temple.

The Bell the bell the B E L L, tell the teacher ah'm no well,
If you're late shut the gate and don't come back till half past eight.

Up and doon the hoose, tae catch a mickey moose,
If ye catch it by the tail, hang it up on a rusty nail.

Mah maw's a millionaire, blue eyes and curly hair, wid ye believe it.
See her walkin doon the street, wae her big banana feet, wid ye believe it.
Sitting amongst the Eskimos, playing a game of dominoes, wid ye believe it.

Not last night but the night before, three wee monkeys came to the door,

Wan wae a fiddle, wan wae a drum and wan wae a pancake stuck tae his bum.

Does yer maw drink wine? Does she drink it aw the time?
Does she get a funny feelin that she's gonny hit the ceiling?

Does yer maw drink gin? Does she drink it oot a tin?
Does she get a funny feelin that's she gonny hit the ceiling?

Murder murder polisman three stairs up,
the wumman in the middle door hit me wae a cup,
Mah nose is aw bleedin, my eye's aw cut,
Murder murder polisman three stairs up.

PK chewing gum
A penny a packet
First you chew it
Then you crack it
Then you stick it in your jacket
PK chewing gum
A penny a packet.

I think o' the days o' my tenement hame,
We've got fancy hooses but they're no just the same,
I'll swap your gisunder, flyovers and jams,
For a tuppenny ride on old Glesga trams.

Gone is the Glasgow that I used to know,
Big Wullie, Wee Shuggy, the steamie the Co,
The skilpit wee bachle, the glaikit big dreep,

Yer baws on the slates, yer gas at a peep.

Those days wurny rosy and money was tight,
The wages half finished oan Saturday night,
But still we came through it and weathered the ruts,
And the reason is simple oor parents had guts.

There she goes, there she goes, peerie heels and pointed toes,
Look at her feet she thinks she's neat, black stockings and dirty feet.

Ah widnae get merrit if ah' wiz you, if I wiz you, if I wiz you,
Ah widnae get merrit if ah' wiz you, ah'd rather stay wae ma mammy.

Clap a clap a handies, Daddy's comin hame,
Penny's in his pocket for his wee wean.

O ye canny shove yer granny aff the bus,
O ye canny shove yer granny aff the bus,
O ye canny shove yer granny, cos she's yer mammy's mammy,
Ye canny shove yer granny aff the bus.

O ye can shove yer other granny aff the bus,
O ye can shove yer other granny aff the bus,
O ye canny shove yer other granny, cos she's yer faither's mammy,
Ye canny shove yer other granny aff the bus.

My maw says Iv'e tae go, wae my faither's dinner o
Beef and totties, stewin steak, wae a wee bit currant cake.

Beatties biscuits are the best, in yer belly they digest,
Doon the lavvy they go west, Beatties biscuits are the best.

Wee chookie burdy trill trill trill, laid an egg on the windae sill,
Then the windae began to crack, wee chookie burdy, quack quack, quack.

Ah'm no hairy Mary ah'm yer maw, ah'm no hairy Mary ah'm yer maw,
Ah'm no hairy Mary, ah'm yer maws canary, ah'm no hairy Mary ah'm yer maw.

Where was Moses when the lights went out?
He was in Sauchiehall Street smoking a dout,
The dout was wee, so was he,
Where was Moses when the lights went out.

Three craws sat upon a wa', sat upon a wa' sat upon a wa',
Three craws sat upon a wa', on a cauld and frosty morning.

The first craw wiz greetin fur his maw, greetin fur his maw, greetin fur his maw,
The first craw wiz greetin fur his maw, on a cauld and frosty morning.

The second craw fell and broke his jaw, fell and broke his jaw, fell and broke his jaw,
The second craw fell and broke his jaw, on a cauld and frosty morning.

The third craw coodny caw at a', coodny caw at a', coodny caw at a',

The third craw coodny caw at a',on a cauld and frosty morning.

And that's a' absolutely a', absolutely a', absolutely a',
And that's a' absolutely a', on a cauld and frosty morning.

Two little dicky birds sitting on a wall, one named Peter one named Paul.
Fly away Peter fly away Paul, come back Peter come back Paul.

Baby's eyes are Irish, baby's eyes are blue,
Baby's like her daddy, his eyes are Irish too,
But daddy's gone to heaven, gone to paradise,
Leaving his beautiful baby, with the beautiful blue Irish eyes.

Oh the big ship sails on the ally ally oh, the ally ally oh, the ally ally oh.
The big ship sails on the ally ally oh, on the first day of September.

Bobby Shafto went to sea, silver buckles on his knee.
He'll come back and marry me, bonnie Bobby Shafto.

Who''ll come intae mah wee hoose, mah wee hoose, mah wee hoose.
Who'll come intae mah wee hoose, and make it a wee bit bigger.

Hey Jock McCuddey, mah cuddie;s up a dyke.
And if you catch mah cuddie, mah cuddie wull gie you a bite.

Ali baba ali baba who's got the baw,
I haven't got it, in my pocket, I haven't got it at aw.

We are three wee gallus girls, sailing out to sea,
And if you pick the fairest one, you're sure to pick me.

A rishy tishy petticoat, a rishy tishy P,
A rishy tishy petticoat, and you're the one for me

Horsey horsey clippity clop, horsey horsey do not stop.
Let your tail go swish and your wheels go round.
Giddy up giddy up we're homeward bound.

Ask no questions, tell no lies,
Keep your mouth shut, and you'll catch no flies.

Ah went tae the pictures the morra, ah took a front seat at the back.
Ah said to the wummin behind me, ah canny see fur yer hat.
She gave me some broken biscuits, ah ate them then gave her them back.
Ah fell fae the stalls tae the balcony, and broke a front bone in mah back.

All of a sudden a big black pudding came flying through the air.
It hit Mrs Kelly right in the belly, and knocked her doon the stair.

Wee Sam, a piece oan jam, went tae London in a pram.
The pram broke whit a joke, wee Sam, a piece oan jam.

If ye should see a fat wummin, staunin at the corner bumming, that's mah mammy.
If ye should see a wee bit trouble, puttin oan a sixpenny double, that's mah mammy.

There was murder last night at the fish shoap, a wee dug stole a haddy bone.
A big dug tried tae take it aff him, so I hut it wae a tottie scone.
I ran tae ma auntie Sara's, and shouted "Auntie Sara, are ye in?"
Her false teeth wur lying oan the table, her hair wis hingin oan a peg.
But I nearly pissed myself laughing, when I saw her screwin aff her widden leg.

Back Court, Kidston Streett/Florence Street (GDC).

Breahead Street, Oatlands (GDC).

Crown Street from Ballater Street, July 1973.

Gorbals Cross, south east corner, July 1973.

Gorbals Street, west side north of Oxford Street, April 1973.

Polmadie Bridge. Bridgeton in the distance (D McCallum).

Rutherglen Road looking east, Polmadie Road, 1995 (NMCN)

Rutherglen Road at Queensferry Street, 1995 (NMCN)

CHAPTER 4

Lynda McGovern

The Lowe Family

I have wonderful memories of the old Oatlands before the decanting and shoddy refurbishment. There were 4 of us, my brother James, my youngest brother Derek and my sister Angela.

The house (we called it a house) was a room and kitchen with outside toilet and no hot water. This was at 19 Roseberry Street and this had been my Grandfather's house where he had brought 5 of a family up, 1 of them being my mother, so she was a real 'Oatcake from Oatlands.'

Our close was between Wullie Scorgie's and Mrs Feeley's Fruit Shop. A a wee bit further was Parkers the Dairy and at the top of the street was Mullholland's Dairy. Facing us was Leslie the Butcher with the best square sausage going.

On a good summers day my da would lean out the windae as we were low down and caw the rope for me and my sister Angela the other end of the rope tied to the lamppost.

Wullie Scorgie's was where 'The Christmas Club' was joined and I remember buying my mum 2 black cats for the fireplace by saving my penny every Saturday. In the summer Mr Scorgie would come out with his brown coat on and pull over the canopy and then you knew it was summer and it was Walls ice cream time.

Mrs Feeley's Fruit Shop had sacks of potatoes and Mrs Feeley would put her rubber gloves on to weigh out your 3lbof potatoes. My mum (ma) would arrange for us four to get an apple and crisps for our dinner all through the summer holidays, and they would get paid on a Friday from Mrs Feeley then it was off to Richmond Park with our picnic.

Rutherglen Road was packed with shops. Miss Winks the Boutique, Frames for the Roller Blinds for the windows and the treat on a Saturday was 'The Oddspot Restaurant' which was actually a cafe, for mince and tatties. A new pair of shoes could be bought from Glendale Footwear Shop.

Facing the shops on Rutherglen Road was the Richmond Park which housed the ducksy, the sandy park with the swing park, and the shows at the Glasgow Fair. Oh the lovely memories now when you look back

On Polmadie Road there was St Margaret's Church right next to a row of shops. There was Curries Newsagents then McCann's shop that sold everything from nylons to nails. The Splash pub and of course the chippy, Marios, which was packed on a Friday night. We always got a chippy tea as Friday was 'The Steamie' night, everything stripped, bedcovers, curtains the lot. ,Saturday morning was hot bath and a towel for the folk that had no bath or inside toilet but 50% of Oatlands had no bath or inside toilet unless you lived in the pre war houses which included Rosyth Street and Granton Street.

When I was 11 we moved from Roseberry Street up to the posher part of Oatlands, Across the way was Shawfield Stadium which was packed on a Friday night, then of course across the road we had the Jennie's Burn which had dirty coloured water running into it from the chemical factory, but all the colours looked glorious to us.

Childhood memories of a place called Oatlands that will always conjure up love in my heart.

Helen Wemyss (Former Rutherglen Road Resident)

Poverty?

It is only recently, since I have managed to regain contact online with all the lovely people from the Old Gorbals, that the realisation hit me that, as poor as the people in the Gorbals were, there still remained a number of levels of poverty within that community.

You had the people that were lucky enough to have more than one or two rooms and an inside toilet in their tenement home. Usually their father was working and kept his family as well fed and clothed as possible. They still struggled to make ends meet but they somehow managed to have a wee holiday for a week or so by the seaside.

Then you had another group, people whose whole families were crammed into either one or two rooms. Their father worked hard and still did his best to keep the family fed and clothed. Life was a real struggle and a day here and there at the seaside was usually their annual treat.

Finally you had another group. These were the people who were not only crammed into one or two bedrooms in a crumbling tenement, but their head of the household was a heavy drinker who thought nothing of drinking all his wages down at the pub on a Friday night, and was often called to go home by one of the weans that his long suffering wife had sent to the pub to fetch him home. The kids would go hungry and cold unless a kind neighbour helped out.

When people get together now and talk about the poverty of the Gorbals they all have very different memories. Some have very happy memories despite their grim surroundings. Others though only remember the abject poverty they suffered as kids, being cold and being hungry most of the time. Often they want nothing more to do with the place and live in resentment.

I was one of the unlucky ones in the last group but that still doesn't prevent me from remembering all that was good about the Gorbals, the wonderful community spirit of the people who lived there, those people that did their best to help each other out, the people who kept a close eye on all the weans in the street.......even those that weren't theirs.

Yes, we might have been poverty stricken but somehow I think growing up in the Gorbals made us all rich in a way that money just can't buy. I believe I am a much better person for having had that experience.

Alice McLaughlin

I was brought up living in number 210 Wolseley Street in Oatlands, Glasgow and around October 1967 when I was only five years old I was involved in an accident that made the front page headlines in the Daily Record newspaper 'Oatlands Girl Saves Baby Brother.'

I was told to wait at the bottom of the close mouth, or close as it was known to us, with my wee baby brother who was ten months old who was lying in his pram while my mammy ran up the stairs of our tenement with her messages.

Being a very helpful wean I started bumping the go-chair up the stairs without her knowing. Halfway up the stairs the sky light glass fell down and apparently I bent over the pram and saved my brother, a sheet of the glass fell on my head while I held onto the pram.

I was taken to the Victoria Hospital to get five stitches put in my head with blood covering my wee woollen suit, the factor gave my mammy a cheque for £25 as it was his responsibility to keep and maintain the building. There was a reporter from the Daily Record newspaper who asked me what I would do with the money and I answered saying I would buy wool and knitting needles to knit a new suit to replace the one ruined with all the blood from my head cut.

That tenement of ours was right above the Molls Mire Pub on the corner of Wolseley Street and Polmadie Road, and like most people we loved our house in Oatlands. I was talk of the playground in my school which was Wolseley Street School and had Logan Street on one side of it and Bilbao Street on the other side.

My maiden name was Turner and back in those days and I loved my school and living in the area playing with all my pals at peever and skipping ropes etc. We had a terrific childhood in those days.

Then when the Gorbals clearance started, Oatlands followed next and our part of Wolseley Street was first to be demolished so we moved to the "Dampies" in Sandiefield Road in the Gorbals although now I live in Cambuslang, but I will always remember when I made the headlines in the newspaper as a five year old. It's just a pity my mammy never kept the newspaper.

Alex O'Neill

These are the memories of a great childhood growing up in the Gorbals and Oatlands. I was born in Rottenrow Hospital and lived at 331 Lawmoor Street and I attended St Francis Primary School and St Bonaventure's Secondary School.

I remember the great days of summer playing fitba' in the street, also playing kick the can and a game of tig, going up to the first floor landing of out tenement building and dreeping from the window down to the back court, although some nutters tried dreeping from the second storey window and got broken legs/bones for their trouble but got a badge of honour for their heroics.

The May Procession with our white shirts and green sashes and the girls dressed up like wee brides, then us boys went to play over in Dixon's Blazes, pinching the detonators for the railway lines and dropping bricks on them till they exploded, while all the time keeping our eyes out for the Rubberneck, as we all knew fine well that he murdered kids.

We used to go to the bridge on Polmadie Road and lean over waiting for the steam engine locomotives to pass below, blowing its steam upwards and covering us in smoke. It was great fun going to the bottom of Polmadie Road/Rutherglen Road and getting hudgies on the rubbish carts which was another deadly Glasgow game but brilliant fun.

I remember Smythes pub in CumberlandStreet. I was sent there many a time to tell my dad to come home and I used to get a penny from my da for going to the Pawn shop on a Monday morning with his suit or the shoes my ma got out of the catalogue at the weekend.

Then I remember we had a telly with a meter that never had any money in it, and of course the padlock was gone as soon as the telly was delivered. One time they came to take it away and my ma and the guy were arguing like hell and the poor guy didn't notice my ma was unscrewing one of the legs then she gave the guy a shove against the telly and it fell onto the floor smashing the screen. Ma told him he could take the telly now and we had another in no time at all as ma couldn't miss Coronation Street.

Then of course we had fights with the next streets, which was always a bit of a highlight, although nothing too serious at that age, thank God. I remember being taken to the Polis Station at Lawmoor Street after playing on a building site with a nail through my welly (as far as I knew) it felt like it was clean through my foot so the Polis called an ambulance while trying to calm me down, and my ma and half the women in Lawmoor Street. They decided to take off my welly to stop any bleeding. I was screaming the place down and my ma was crying and yelling, but they managed to get my welly off. There was no blood and the nail was only just touching my foot, it hadn't penetrated my foot at all, What a letdown for everyone, and I got a clipped ear for crying like a baby and a slapped ear for playing on a building site in the first place.

I remember one night when we were flitting to a new tenement house. We were using a wheelbarrow and carrying other household belongings in our arms, as we were only moving a few closes along the street. We had did the same when we moved to Florence Street, although moving to Polmadie Road was a good bit further away in Oatlands and we got a lorry to help the move. We lived by the pen when we moved to Polmadie Road which had a bakery and I used to go down in the morning, or my da did, before work and get hot rolls. I always asked da to get burnt ones (the best).

I used to love going over to Richmond Park for the swings or the pond with the swans (the ducksy) and of course when the shows came to Glasgow Green it was just the best place on earth, just jumping on the rides, who needed money lol, or if you were very lucky you got a wee job at the shows during the daytime.

The highlight for me was going to Parkhead on a Saturday or midweek to watch Celtic play and it was a sheer joy getting my scarf ready (making sure it was clean) and going to Gorbals Cross to to try and get a lift on one of the supporters buses, getting to the park and asking "Mister can you give me a lift over please?" (In those far off days a man could lift his son or another boy over the turnstile for free) then when inside the ground standing there with thousands of other Celtic supporters and singing all our songs. I don't think that any other team has the support that we do.

At Christmas time I just loved going over to Argyle Street in the 'toon' and seeing all the windows lit up with those flashing lights. I used to love looking through the windows at all the toys on show. Glasgow at Christmas time was something special, and Lewis's store was a dream come true for us weans with the toy department.

Then playing on the banks of the River Clyde, occasionally "borrowing" one of the nellies (bogey carts) and having races with your pals all around the docks hoping none of the men would shout at you to stop!!!.

My ma and her sister worked in one of the whisky bonds and used to come back home at night and remove the half bottles they had hidden in their knickers and against their thighs as they could not be searched there. They would fill some of the larger bottles with the whisky and take the now empty half bottles (needs must) back with them for the following days shift, and repeat the process.

Then with the Gorbals clearance of the old tenement buildings we had the emergence of the high rise buildings in the soo-side, and these were monstrous looking. To me they heralded the end of an era of my life and everybody else's time in the soo-side of old, where we had so many great days. By this time we had moved house to Florence Street then onwards to Weir Street in Tradeston, but then returned once more to Florence Street.

Then I became of working age and joined the Merchant Navy (like a lot of Gorbals boys), but I will always remember Glasgow as a very tough place to be brought up, but also a place where neighbours would take you in to their homes with open arms, where everybody knew each other and women stood in closes at night and gabbed. Men got drunk together but most of all the weans were loved unconditionally.

I am returning to Glasgow later this year (2015) but I doubt that I will recognise the place too much. I will still love it though, as I have always done, and when people out here in New Zealand where I now live ask where we come from, we always say with pride, "I belong to Glasgow." May she flourish safely.

Gerry Mcaleavy

It was a day like any other getting up for school and walking there. St John Bosco's new school was getting built then, and the old ground was used by the workmen for all their machinery, dumper trucks, fork lift trucks etc and everyday as I walked by here, I would see men starting up the dumper truck which I had become quite fond of. I used to watch them start it up and go about their business.

It was mainly Saturdays when I watched them and they really took my attention. I could stand there for ages fascinated looking at them while thinking to myself "I can drive that I know I can." One Saturday as usual I went down there and lo and behold there wasn't a sound coming from the workmen's area, just complete silence, which indicated for some reason the men weren't working that day. Great!!!

"Now's my chance" I thought, to have a go at this dumper truck. I got through the fencing alright and approached the truck with caution, just in case a watchman was about, but nope, not one person in sight, so I went over to the truck and by luck, the starting handle was still in its position. I was eleven years old and this was my biggest adventure. I turned the starting handle, phut, phut, phut, and then nothing. I took a harder turn of the handle phut, phut, phut, and again nothing.

I tried a good few more times, each time more determined than the last, phut, phut, phut, brrrrr. Bingo, it started up and was running so I jumped in the seat and took off while pressing all the handles to see how it worked, and the bucket was tipping up and down brilliant!!! I drove around for a wee while in the workmen's area thinking I was Jackie Stewart the racing car driver lol.

Then I thought "I'm gonny take this thing down the street" so I crashed it through the fence turning into Logan Street, then turned left into Wolseley Street. It was such a great feeling. I was actually driving this machine that I had dreamed of so many weeks before . As I drove down the street I slowed right down because there were weans playing who were about five or seven years old and they were shouting out for a hurl.

So I tipped the bucket down to let them step into it and once they were in I lifted the bucket up and on our merry way we went, turning up into Elmfoot Street then into Kilbride Street and then back down Logan Street with all the kids in the bucket. Then my mum, 'big Joyce' appeared from a close and stopped the proceedings, making me lower the bucket and letting the weans step out. She then asked me had I crashed the concrete on the fence and I said "No", and she said "You're a friggin liar because you were seen doing it" and she made me drive it back to where I had got it from.

The police came to our house an hour later and cautioned me, and I was sent to a Children's Panel for my stupidity, which I now see with the help of hind-sight, but to us kids everything was an adventure, and those wee weans in the bucket had a great adventure that day, and I think they will always remember that day.

My punishment was being kept in for a week but I used to lock the bathroom door and climb out the window and climb down the drainpipe and into the street to play football with the rest of the boys. My mum thought I was in the bedroom until she heard my voice in the street, then up the window would go and she'd be shouting at me to "Get up the stair smartish." I didn't listen to her, and just played on until my dad just whistled "Gerry up!!!" I then went up straight away, but never once did he hit me, it was always "Dae whit yer maw tells ye." "Aye right da" I would reply, but I never did.

Christina Gray

I was born in Kidston Street, Gorbals, Glasgow. We then moved to Oatlands to Roseberry Street, and then onto Dalmeny Street, so the Gorbals and Oatlands was my upbringing and was thoroughly enjoyed by myself and all my pals.

My ma would often say "On ye go and out to play with you and down the back court." I would happily go and stay there playing with all my wee friends as we played Chinese ropes with rubber bands and we used to see how high we could jump, and then doing handstands against the wall. Then like all girls in the soo-side we would play balls, bouncing them off the tenement walls until an angry neighbour would chase us away as the noise was too much!!!

We would play shops in the back court and smash up glass to use as "cash" and we'd use an old newspaper to wrap our "mince" (which was old clabber or mud) and sell it to our customers ha ha, boy did we have fun and laughter when we were weans.

Friday was "Steamie" day and time for a hot bath also. My ma would love all the banter with all the other women doing their weekly wash and I wonder today how all our mothers managed without all the mod cons that we all take for granted nowadays. In between keeping us weans all neatly dressed, and the house was clean without the aid of suction hoovers and microwave ovens etc, and not forgetting having spotlessly clean net curtains hanging on the windows, and the most important job was taking their turn of "washing the stairs".

Sometimes in the back court you would have someone playing an accordion and us weans would all gather round and listen with glee, and then us weans would end up dancing to the tunes, but before we left we gave the accordionist a farthing.

On Friday nights my da would come in the house with a big brown bag full of chocolate and other goodies for us weans. It's special things like these that we never forget in our great bringing up in the soo-side, and we have so many happy memories to cherish.

One thing that does stick in my mind and that is when I was ten years old I went sleep walking. I must have come down three flights of stairs and crossed the road then I woke up banging on my mum's pals window. What a shock for my ma and da who never heard me leaving the hoose lol.

Elizabeth Kelly

I was born at home in Salisbury Street in the Gorbals.

Just like many other children at that time of the old tenements, my story goes my mum goes into labour and the midwife arrives at our house. Now the lady who was the midwife was actually an African and with no racist thought or I assume no knowledge of racism, my dad used to describe this lady "as black as the coal in the bunker".

My dad was sent out, as was the custom in those days, while mum got on with the delivery. When dad returned the nurse handed me to him and he nearly passed out. His first vision of me was of the left side of my head wrapped in a bandage.

I was not disfigured. 'Don't be alarmed' my smiling face told my dad. The nurse said she has one ear that's sticking out and that's why she had bandaged it, so as to rectify the problem!!!. As you can imagine my dad was relieved, however for years my family would talk about this story, with I'm sure the usual Gorbals banter.

Me, I spent my youth believing I had an ear which stuck out, although now I wonder to this day did this well meaning African midwife get it right lol.

Ann McLaughlin

My granny lived at the corner of Cumberland Street and Gorbals Street, facing the Granite City and it was a great house as it had windows in both streets, and we were always hinging oot watching the world go buy. My granny was always hingin oot the windae and could tell you who went in and out of the pub - time in and time out. You could see right down to Gorbals Cross and along Cumberland Street and then to Eglinton Street. I think she had one of the best views in the Gorbals.

One time me and my pal Cath (R.I.P) who lived in Cally Road (Caledonia Road) decided to go to my aunty's house in Helensburgh as my uncle was the janitor for Rhu Yatching Club, so unbeknown to them we went out in a rowing boat and could not get back to shore. We just went round and round and had to take of our knickers to wave and had to get the Rescue Boat to tow us back in. My aunt and uncle were not very happy and we never went back again.

Also when we where wee, we used to play Kiss, Kick or dare and I kicked the can and took my big toe nail off, and if we got kissed, there was one guy, who I will not name, that none of us would kiss, and we pretended that we were sick or had to go home. Such a shame for the guy.

Between Florence Street and Crown Street, the posh street in the back, there was a big shiny tile thing that went the full length of 3/4 closes and is was so slippy we used to dare people to run across it, but normally we used to shuffle along it on our bums, but there was still many a broken bone falling of it.

I also remember the couch beds you used to get that spring loaded and made up into a couch. When I was a baby my granny was watching me in Cumberland Street and put me in the one in the big room, as we called it. My old granda came in wi' a wee drink in him and when my granny went to get me she could not find me and asked auld Sammy "Where's the babe?" He said "Sure I don't know?" He had just shut up the bed/couch with me in it lol

Helen Ann Congalton

Oh I remember well our room n kitchen (and inside toilet) in Florence Street. We were the last close before Dixon's Blazes. I never thought of Dixon's Blazes as a frightening place, maybe because we were so close. There was me Helen Mortimer, my sister Theresa, and our mum n dad, Nellie and Davie. We had roaring coal fires in both rooms and we also had a big tin bath filled with water which was boiled in kettles on the stove. In front of the kitchen fire was where we had our baths. I loved it.

My mum got a TV in 1953 and as I got older our house was always full with our pals in watching 'The Lone Ranger,' 'Davey Crocket', 'Champion the Wonder Horse' and loads more, but the biggest enjoyment we had was when mum closed over the big wooden shutters on the windows got us Wall's ice cream, sat around the coal fire and would tell us ghost stories. She was a wonderful story teller and would speak in a low voice until near the end and then shout BOO! Oh we would all jump about screaming.

Christmas time was magic and a visit to Lewis's was a must. Oh I can still remember the excitement of seeing Santa climbing and then the long wait all the way up the stairs till we got to the floor with the grotto. Then a few nights before Christmas we would go to Cumberland Street. The hustle and bustle of all the shoppers was wonderful. Everyone was happy and I can still smell that beautiful scent of tangerines.

We entertained ourselves back then playing beds, ropes, kick the can and playing baws. Then we would announce we were having a concert. Rehearsals would begin and they were taken so seriously you would have thought we were pop stars haha. Crepe paper was bought in abundance, every colour you could think of. Skirts were made, as were shawls and hats. The venue was the old washhouse (midden) out the back at number 353 Florence Street. The auld chimney stack was our microphone. And the audience was all the mammies chairs borrowed from every house; all seated "Let the Show Begin.

𝒍𝒍𝒍𝒍𝒍𝒍𝒍𝒍𝒍𝒍

"Hello everybody Hello. We're here to open the show, there'll be singing and dancing and lots of romancing. Hello everybody, hello."

We danced and sang with all our hearts and of course the grand finale was "I once had a dear auld mother" and there wisnae a dry eye in the hoose.

The highlight of my young life in the Gorbals was making my First Holy Communion at St Francis. I still recall the preparation and mum had my dress made by a lady in Caledonia Road. It was a wonderful day. I can still remember exactly where I sat and the hymns we sang and how nervous I was. Then it was off for breakfast to Errol Street and on to Jerome's to have my picture taken.

The May Procession was the icing on the cake. We followed the May Queen round the streets into St Francis and the May Queen would be crowned to the wonderful sound of voices singing "O Mary We Crown Thee with Blossoms Today, Queen of the Angels and Queen of the May."

I have so many memories of the Gorbals these are just a few, I hope you enjoyed my sharing them with you.

Mary Higgins

Growing up with five sisters and one brother in Hutchesontown Court in the Gorbals my parents never had much money, so when my three eldest sisters were out working it was great, as my other sister and I would love having a wee catwalk show while they were out.

One day one of my sister's was working hard in the Twomax Knitwear Factory building when I decided to wear her new clothes to school. As soon as she had left for work I ran upstairs and got all dolled up thinking that I really looked hot, even wearing her brand new knickers (5 pairs for a £1) out of that famous Candleriggs Market.

At lunch time I ran fast all the way home so I could change the "evidence" before she got home, but she had got home first. Well she went mental shouting and screaming at me and when she realised I had on her knickers she started screaming at me outside in the street "Get my knickers aff!" I was pure mortified as the other schoolkids were walking past the house for lunch. I never did that again lol.

I left Hutchensontown Court (my folks still live there) to go and live in Logan Street in Oatlands when I was twenty one years old although I now live in Blantyre.

Jean Friel

I was born in 1949 and brought up in Wolseley Street in Oatlands.

My early memories include going to the Ritz Picture Hall to see 'Calamity Jane' and must have seen it a few times because I used to sing the "Deadwood Stage" to everybody up our close.

I remember going to a cafe which I'm sure was called 'The Top Hat.' It was on Rutherglen Road and also along Rutherglen Road I used to go to the "sonny pon" in Richmond park with my mum. Another great memory is of standing at the hot steamie wall and it was great in winter time getting your hands warmed there with all the other boys and girls swapping stories.

We then moved to the Gorbals in Orchard Street, which was in between Gilmour Street and Moffat Street, just across from the 'Harmony Bar.' I loved our wee room and kitchen and my mammy kept it lovely, cosy and warm.

One Sunday my aunt and cousin were visiting us and me and Tricia were out playing when we spotted a big piece of rope hanging from one of the dykes. We decided to take it off and the next thing a big line of washing fell on to the muddy ground, well my cousin and me ran into the swing park there and stayed there for a long time. We never told anyone it was us but I did hear the lady was going mental looking for the culprits.

I had a good wee pal called Mary McNulty and her dad was a coalman. One night my ma took both of us to the Ritz Picture House and as Mary stayed in Rutherglen we would take her home. When we got to the bottom of her close, she would go upstairs and she would shout out when she had reached her door, but this night there was a terrible scream so we ran up the stairs (albeit me hiding behind my ma). Guess what it was that had frightened her? A big cat lying on the window ledge. All the neighbours must have thought there was a murder the way Mary was screaming.

I loved my life living in the Gorbals with my lovely mum, dad and brothers and we had relatives all around us with great neighbours. We moved to Easterhouse in 1960 but that's another story.

We couldn't stay away though, my dad went back there to work as a caretaker in 1977 and was there till he died in 2011.

Molly Dooley

My first outstanding memory as a child was starting school, my da took me. The teacher appeared to be giant, her name was Miss Heslin. My da was five foot eight inches and Miss Heslin was taller than him, and she wore nice shiny shoes, brogues, a dark red colour. For some reason I did not start at the usual intake date with the other five year olds, and the term was well on its way. Miss Heslin whispered to me that it was her first day too she was taking over from Miss McCartney. I was glad because Miss McCartney looked REALLY old and because of her straight rigid back and the way she walked, I felt fearful of her. She stayed for one week with Miss Heslin and I was right, she was strict, putting children in the corner for talking and shouting and threatening to lock the children in the cupboard.

My da continued to take me to school before he went to work. He was a docker and one wee boy said my da looked like a tramp. I am assuming this was because of his work clothes, anyway, I punched him around the ears and he ran away crying so I got a letter and my da had to go and speak to the teacher. That was the first of many letters.

When my da's work shifts changed my big brothers had to take me and they didn't want to be bothered with a daft wee lassie, and they tried to lose me going through back courts and over dykes and railings and they were amazed that I climbed and scrambled and dreeped and kept up with them.

It was after school the real adventures began as they went over the mollsy mire and jumped over the burn they played Cowboys and they found "balloons" for me to play with and told me to blow them up. The "balloons" we're smelly, I filled them with dirty water from the burn and threw them at my brothers, as they ran away laughing. Jack, two years older was wounded and Jon found a blood stained rag and tied it round Jack's head, it had two wee strings at each end, other times they would tie the blood stained rags onto branches to make flags. This is quite horrifying now, but that is how we played in the 1950's. I was 18 before I learned what these balloons were, my husband to be had some, he told me he got them free with my engagement ring.

My brothers moved up to the big playground and continued going over the mollsy going up to the railway carriages, the goods wagons, and nicking small packages being delivered from catalogue. I was making my own friendships then. A big crowd of us all going whatever way, we heard the shouts"A BARNEY A BARNEY" and we would run in that direction to watch boys fighting, no wrestling on the telly then, in fact no telly. I got kept in as I was told to keep away from fights. I climbed and done big jumps from dyke to dyke and climbed trees, made a rope swing, always getting injuries, my mother who had ten boys at the time always said she would rather have another ten boys than another one of me .

Me and my pals pulled all the bins out of a midden (a bin shelter) and were making a den in a backcourt in Rutherglen Road when the whole shelter fell in on us. An ambulance and fire brigade were there and five of us were taken to hospital, we were trapped under the debris and choking with dust. I got kept in as I had been warned about the danger of these middens.

We were still in primary when we would go into a midden in a back court from a pub and get boxes of sawdust and throw them over each other, and we would get tin taps from beer bottles in these middens and pry the cork from the back of them to make badges. We would cover our cardigans and jerseys with these brightly covered tin tops and do the backs of our jumpers for each other. One evening we were doing this and a man was watching us. He said he knew a back court where there was hundreds of tin tops and he would take me and my pal, we said we were going home as we were hungry, he then offered to buy us chips. Well instinct prevailed and I shouted to a woman at her window. Her man and other young men came charging after him, chased him through the backs jumping railings, they chased him from the back of The Braehead Bar all the way up the Oatlands and kicked his head in. Unfortunately, by the time they got up to him it was the wrong guy, that guy was looking for his dog. I got kept in again.

I tried to behave. I was to come straight home and say prayers to Immaculate Mary and as I did not listen in school my mother heard my prayer saying "Him I too late Mary" instead of "Immaculate Mary." She REALLY despaired of me, so I was told to pray to my guardian angel where for 'Fold thy wings round me' I was saying "Fold diamonds round me" and "Our father who farts in heaven." My mother was in a tizzy, I never got kept in again. She was saying to my father that I did not even know the "Our Father" and he tried to teach me to say 'Hallowed be thy name' and I would repeat "Hello, what's you name." I was so much a pest.

I could go on and on, I remember when I got attacked in Florence Street and fought off my attacker; my brothers saved a family who's house was on fire; the police brutality at the time; my da losing his leg; how I became a good Catholic and still am; how my mother was not letting me go to Holyrood because she couldn't afford the uniform and the neighbours in our street got together and got me my uniform, briefcase and beret, and trench coat from Black and Campbell.'

It does not matter where we came from, we enjoyed the journey.

Gary Moore

I was born and raised in the Gorbals. Growing up in Queen Elizabeth Square in the 1970's was a rough and tumble affair.

In the early days, the corridors had no doors on them, and living in the 'big block' (B & C block) the length of the corridors seemed to go on for miles when we were riding our 'Choppers' along them, or playing with our 'Evil Knievel' toys on their motorbikes. Thomas Kennedy (TC) was the king of the Chopper gang, he was the one who could do all the tricks, wheelies and stunts, he was like the Evil Knievel of The Gorbals!

We never just played in the corridors though, we also played outside to give our Ma and Da's some well earned 'peace." We loved playing at the bottom of the blocks, in the Rose Garden (The Rosey), at the 'jumps' on Ballater place, the swing park complete with sky high chute, and the ramps at the Cumberland Arcade. On a windy day the wind would be so strong around Queen Elizabeth, we would stand at the swing park and watch people's washing flying from their verandahs, and sometimes even the verandah doors would blow off as people rushed out to get their washing in!

Sometimes though, we engaged in more dangerous pursuits, and thinking back it's a wonder we made it out in one piece. One of the most dangerous things I ever saw was my friend Peter Innes (INNY) and my brother Stephen Moore (PUD) making a swing in a verandah on the 8th floor, swinging right outside the building from one end of the verandah to the other hundreds of feet up, and we thought it was great, not giving a second thought to the danger!

Another dangerous game was climbing down the shafts of the refuge chute on a rope. Myself and my friends John Gallagher (GAL) and Thomas Curran, we climbed down the rope from one landing to another, but the walls were so smelly and dirty that we never tried it again, also we had to do it at night in case we got rubbish tipped over us from the floors above!

One of the things we found great fun was to buy gherkins out of Anne's Fry and Marios and throw them into The Elizabethan pub, (taking care not to get caught by our Ma's and Da's who drank in there!) haha we didn't really know what gherkins were and it seemed to be a local craze to throw them into 'The Lizzy' , which was kinda amusing when you were a kid!

I loved my childhood in Queen Elizabeth Square, and when we moved to the Calton in the early 80's I really missed it. Not long after I moved out I was coming home from hanging about with my friends in Hutchesontown Court when I absent mindedly just automatically headed to Queen Elizabeth and right up to my house on the 6th floor and walked into my old house. The man who had moved in thankfully knew who I was. He looked at me in amusement from his armchair and said "Son.....you don't live here anymore!"

I have such great memories of growing up in the Gorbals and always missed Queen Elizabeth Square. I would like to dedicate my story to my dear friends who I grew up with who are no longer here, they are sadly missed and I'm so glad I shared so many great times with them.......we really were Gorbals Diehards, and I'm always proud of where I grew up.

Josephine O'Boyle

I was born at 143 Aikenhead Road, Govanhill, Glasgow, about a mile from the Gorbals and I moved to the Gorbals when I was about 8 years of age to 20 Pine Place to the infamous "Dampies" (aka' Hutchie E'). Having come from a tenement to a brand new built house to me was so exciting. Although in our tenement we were lucky enough to have an inside toilet, this new build house also had running hot water, a bathroom, and for me, the luxury of all luxuries, I got a bedroom to myself, which was great as in our tenement I had slept in the bed recess in the kitchen. "The Dampies" consisted of 12 blocks of deck access flats, which contained 1, 2 and 3 bedroom flats.

Being so young I wasn't initially aware of the problems with dampness in our new house. I just remember the big long adjoining corridors where all the children would play. As a young girl it wasn't unusual to chap someone's door if you knew they had a baby in the house and ask to take their baby a walk "round the block." "The block" for where I stayed was 20 Pine Place, then onto 50 Pine Place, then 80 Pine Place, then 155 Crown Street and that took me back to 20 Pine Place, it went round in an adjoining square. It was something I done quite often and I can't believe now how easily mothers handed their babies over to young girls to walk in their pram, but that's just how it was back then.

Very soon after moving into our new house there were problems with condensation and dampness. Although the dampness in our house was quite bad, we were luckier than some whose houses were really bad with dampness. I knew one family of 2 parents and 5 children, and even though they had a 3 bedroom house, all 7 of them ended up sleeping in the same bedroom, choosing to sleep in the "driest" of all 3 bedrooms in their house for the sake of their health. The dampness problem in those houses was so bad that it wasn't unusual to have mould/fungus growing on the walls or to literally have condensation running down your walls as that's how bad it was for most, if not all, tenants.

After years of tenants fighting with Glasgow City Council and going on a "rent strike" it was decided that "Hutchie E" would be bulldozed and all families were then moved out of the Dampies.

Alexander Neil

Gorbals Living in the 1930's and 1940's

PREFACE

My name is Alexander Neil and I started this story in February 2013 and finished the basic story in November 2013 at age 80 but kept adding things I've later remembered till now, January 2015!

The purpose of this story is to give my stagnating brain something to do and attempt to show my grandchildren and great-grandchildren the huge difference between the living and social conditions of the 1930's and 40's and the present day. I don't profess to be a writer and I don't intend this to be a story about *me*, it's more of a snapshot of life as I experienced it in the 1930's and 1940's. I'll try not to make it too boring. It may only be of interest to my younger relatives and anyone who may be curious about living conditions in Gorbals in the title period.

THE GORBALS

I was born in the Gorbals District of Glasgow in 1933 and I think I had better start by giving people a brief 'glimpse' of the Gorbals as it was then. I won't try to give a history of the Gorbals, there are plenty of old photographs, books and articles about that and they are readily available on the internet. I have read a few 'non-fiction' books about the Gorbals but all they seemed to focus on was violence and drunks. Everything seemed concentrated on negative aspects with very little positive views in these books and in my opinion, some negative things exaggerated!

When Gorbals is mentioned people who never lived there have a look of disdain on their face because of things they have heard or read about Gorbals. I've no doubt there must have been abject poverty in some places, (*Not just in Gorbals*) but I never saw it or perhaps never recognised it. I want to show that things weren't all like that and that the Gorbals had a majority of decent living, hard working, neighbourly and friendly people. That is why so many people today have happy memories of family life in the Gorbals and I am one of them. You can see more fights and drunks now on a Saturday night or morning when the Night Clubs close (*albeit in the city centre where the clubs are and not in the Gorbals*) because people can AFFORD to get drunk more often now. There were (*and still are*) always people who would spend too much money in a pub or bookies to the detriment of their families. It angered me if I saw a man leaving a pub and I knew some member of his family had holes in their shoes! Some men would bleat "*I've worked hard all week and deserve a drink at the weekend*"! Fortunately my father wasn't one of them and fortunately he was a non-drinker and never kept any alcohol in the house. If whisky was required for Medicinal purposes (*e,g, making a 'toddy' for someone*) you could take an empty bottle down to a pub and the barman would put a Gill of whisky in the bottle and charge you accordingly. No need to buy a full bottle of any size.

CONDITIONS THEN AND NOW

Thinking back to these days I also wonder about the fact that the first thing a family had to do at that time was pay their rent. If you didn't, or couldn't pay your rent, then after the usual obligatory warnings you were evicted, so paying rent was the priority, food being a close second. There was no '*Housing*' or '*Council Tax Benefit*' in those days and I wonder, if there weren't any of these benefits now, how many more of today's homes would look like '*slums*'? Sadly there are plenty of houses today all over Britain that look like slums, at least on the inside!

AIR POLLUTION

Glasgow, like lots of other big cities in Britain, was an industrial city and consequently, lots of smoke was generated by factory chimneys and home fires which were fuelled by coal. This deposited a fine coat of dirt and soot on all of the buildings in the city. This slowly built up over the years and stonework on buildings became very black or dark looking. This gave the tenement buildings a rather sombre appearance. The Clean Air Act 1956 was an Act of the Parliament of the United Kingdom. It was in effect until 1964. It introduced '*smoke control areas*' in some towns and cities in which only *smokeless* fuels could be burned. By shifting homes sources of heat towards cleaner coals, electricity, and gas, it reduced the amount of smoke pollution and sulphur dioxide from household fires.

SMOG

Smog is a type of air pollutant. The word "smog" was made in the early 20th century as a portmanteau of the words '*smoke and fog*' to refer to smoky fog through which you could hardly see. It was also dangerous to health and caused a number of deaths to vulnerable people. In the late 1970's and 80's (*I'm not sure of the date*) sandblasting of prominent buildings in the city centre was undertaken to remove years of soot and dirt. Some tenements not scheduled for demolition were also sandblasted.

THE GANGS

I won't dwell on the Gorbals Gangs other than to say, "Yes, they were there" and bad things happened to some people over the years but fortunately, not to anyone that I knew. I didn't have any serious trouble with them when I was young. I managed to avoid serious conflict with them by using a combination of common sense, cowardice, adrenalin rush and a pair of legs that could move like pistons when I felt threatened! (*That's where the adrenalin rush comes in!*)

A big difference from then and now is that where I stayed, no gang 'member' would harm or rob an old person. In fact they would 'pay a visit' to anyone who had! Elderly people could go to the shops without the fear of being robbed or harmed. I had to run a few times to get out of trouble though. Regarding the Glasgow razor gangs. Lord Carmont, a City Judge in the 1950s, came on the scene and handed down some stiff sentences and is credited for curbing some of the gang actions at the time. I believe that more young people who are *not* in gangs are carrying knifes now!

I know a lot of old people say *"this and that didn't happen in my day"*, well they are right, it didn't happen! The big problem now is the widespread use of illegal habit-forming drugs. Drug taking and the amount of cash needed to feed the habit is responsible for serious criminality of all kinds and affects people of all ages and classes. This wasn't known when I was young. With the exception of smoking, I never heard of, or knew of, anyone who took drugs when I was young. I should also add that there wasn't the same problem with lots of young people 'binge' drinking and the various costs of dealing with that! There wasn't a problems with wide-spread obesity either because children played outdoors most of the time and people mostly did manual work and walked a lot of the time, including daily walking up and down stairs in the tenements! Plus we had 'Food Rationing.' I'm not talking about specific cases, I'm talking about situations "in general". I'm not trying to say that things were better then, but life was simpler and less complicated. Quality of life is obviously much, much better now and young children of today are much taller, healthier *and* very knowledgeable for their age.

ON WITH THE STORY

It may be of interest to some people to know that the Gorbals has medieval origins and was at one time Glasgow's Leper Colony. HOSPITAL STREET is formed upon the site of St Ninian's Leper Hospital founded by Lady Lochow in 1350. The Gorbals District is situated on the south bank of the River Clyde, Glasgow's principle river which flows roughly east to west through the city. Our home was in Hospital Street which ran roughly north to south, the north end of the street terminating at Adelphi Street, which ran alongside the river and the south end terminating (*I think, it may have been Cavendish St.*) at Cathcart Road where an 'A' listed building (*a church, now an empty shell*) by Alexander 'Greek' Thomson still stands. I was surprised to recently find out that the tenement building beside the church in Hospital Street was also designed by Alexander Thomson. Hospital Street had a wonderfully smooth surface and it was great for roller skating, go-carts and cycling! After regeneration of the Gorbals only a small part of Hospital Street remains.

The remaining section is the north end of the street. i.e. near the River Clyde, last time I looked, but this may have changed.

The tenement buildings in the Gorbals were mainly built as four, three storey high blocks forming a rectangle, the space in the centre of the rectangle being the back courts where the rubbish bins were kept in three sided roofed enclosures (*which we called 'middens'*). In some cases there was also a 'wash-house' in the back court. There were also metal posts for attaching ropes to hang washing on. (*There were also used for beating carpets, if you had any!*) The courts were separated by walls (*which we called 'dykes'*) and we climbed them repeatedly. If there was a telephone pole next to the wall you could climb to the top of the wall and slide down the pole. Great fun! (*Beware of jagged slivers of wood!*) We also jumped from wall to wall or wall to the roofs of the middens etc. (*In addition, air raid shelters which were built in some back courts in WW2*). If there was a set of railings with spiked tops beneath you as you jumped it was called a 'Death' jump. If a wall was too high to jump from, you had to 'd*reep*' from it. 'Dreeping' involved hanging from the wall by your fingertips and then letting go.

We had 'Back-Court Singers' in these days. These were persons (*usually men*) who were down on their luck and would appear in the back courts and sing simple songs for a few coppers or a sandwich. The sandwich was wrapped in paper and usually thrown from the window to the singer. If they were lucky they would be told to come up the stairs and get a sandwich and a cup of tea. They sat on the stairs to consume their food; they didn't get in to the house.

There were also 'Rag Men' who came round the streets with hand carts or horse drawn carts calling "*Crockery for rags*" or "*Balloons for rags*'. Many a still usable piece of clothing would disappear from a house and a child would suddenly, as if by magic, acquire a balloon!

Going back to the rubbish bins. The bins were very large and the contents (*mostly ashes from the coal fires*) were shovelled in to large baskets and the baskets carried on the backs of the 'Bin Men' out to the street and emptied into a horse drawn cart during the night. I think the workmen had a 'Carbide' lamp (*which had a burning flame*) on the front of their hats. Hard work, but that's how things were in those days! Think of the coal delivery men repeatedly carrying bags of coal up all of the stairs in the tenements! Some coal supply companies gave their customers a fairly large coloured card which the customer displayed in their tenement window if they wanted a delivery. Each company had a different coloured card which was about the size of a Sash Window pane. The stairs to the houses were accessed via a ground level entrance which we called a 'close' and each close had a number. This number, plus your street name of course, being your address. Entering the close and proceeding upstairs brought you to the first landing, upstairs again to the next landing and so on till you reached the third. Each landing usually had three houses on it, meaning there were nine families living up each close and sometimes another two families at ground level.

In most cases you could also enter the close and walk straight through to the back court. If I remember rightly, in some tenement blocks when you reached a landing on the stairs there was only one door. When you opened the door there was a hall, or lobby as we called it, giving access to other residential doors. The lobby (*being warm*) was a favourite with 'down and outs' who had no place to sleep. They made themselves as comfortable as they could and slept there during the night. We called them 'Lobby Dossers'. If you were going out for an early start in the morning, opening the door and seeing a body lying on the doormat could more than startle you! It was not unusual in those days for families to have eight or more children and obviously there were lots of people living in a small area and the population of Glasgow in 1939 was over one million. It's just over six hundred thousand now. (*More info in appendix*)

INFO FROM INTERNET

In 1930's/40's Britain's children were born into a dangerous world. Every year, thousands died of infectious diseases like pneumonia, meningitis, tuberculosis, diphtheria, and polio. Skin problems like scabies and impetigo were common. Infant mortality - deaths of children before their first birthday - was around 1 in 20. From 1945 more vaccines were developed to control childhood diseases. After the war the health of children was generally better than at any other time in history. Vaccines against polio, measles and rubella were developed in the 1950's and 1960's.

There were many nationalities in the Gorbals including lots of Irish and a strong Jewish community. I read an article which said that between 6000 and 9000 Jews stayed in the Gorbals at one time. I've heard the Gorbals Cross area was nick-named *'Little Jerusalem'*. Many local shops and businesses had Jewish owners. As they prospered they moved out to Pollokshields to live but still had businesses in Gorbals. There was a large Synagogue, called The Great Synagogue, in South Portland Street near the Gorbals Library. My mother's sister 'Jean Bain' and her family lived in the building opposite. There was a newspaper called 'The Jewish Echo' available then. The *'Sample Shoe'* shop at the corner of Hospital Street and Old Rutherglen Road was owned by a Jewish man, Mr. Barnett, originally from Russia I believe. (*That shop was later called 'Concorde'*). Another Jewish man, Mr. Jackman, (*or Checkman*) had a small and rather famous shop under the railway bridge which crossed over Cleland Street between Hospital Street and Gorbals Street. He roasted and sold peanuts and toffee apples etc and kept his stock around the corner in a disused shop in Hospital Street. He also took a folding table to Fairgrounds to sell his produce. I went to assist him once to a Fair somewhere in Springburn, on the left hand side of the main road. I can't remember if I got paid with cash or some of his produce and didn't care. I'd been taken to a Fair! The delicious aroma coming from his shop was hard to resist as you passed it!

In our Close we had Irish Catholics, Jews and Protestants and we all lived in harmony. When we were young went to our Church or Sunday School and there was never any mention of divisions of religion in our home. I remember, as a young boy, (*about 11*) being asked at one time by two older boys if I was a *'Billy or a Dan or an old Tin Can'* and I had no idea what these persons were talking about! Someone had to explain to me that I was being asked if I was a Protestant, a Catholic or a Jew. I have never been interested in what anyone's religion was. If they were decent persons that was all I cared about.

Cafés and Fish & Chip Shops were mainly owned by Italians or persons of Italian descent. When Italy entered the war as allies of Germany on 10th June 1940, a large number of these establishments had windows smashed by locals in towns and cities all over Britain, Glasgow I believe being particularly bad!

I've seen many photographs and films depicting the slums of Glasgow, showing dirty houses and permanently dirty children, but the houses of my friends and family were clean (*as were the children*). All three flights of stairs, landings and windows in our Close for example, were washed twice a week by neighbours on a rota basis. You don't see many people doing that nowadays! Neighbours also cleaned them for any elderly, ill or infirm persons who lived beside us and who were unable to do so themselves. Being a close knit community, there was always plenty of people willing to help neighbours when required. There was plenty of overcrowding though with large families in small houses. The largest number of family members to stay in our home at any one time was eight, these being my Mum and Dad, myself and five other surviving siblings, but I know of some houses where there were 12 persons. At that time we didn't consider our houses to be 'slums' but they were miles behind today's standards. Some houses in Abbotsford Place for example, were grand affairs when first built in the mid 1800's, having seven or eight rooms I believe! Sadly they too became 'run down'. People were poor so thick vegetable soup was a staple family food. (*As was 'Stovies', a sort of hotpot*). Some women would be worried because they were having another child and wondered how they would cope with an even larger family and invariably someone would say, "*Just put more water in the soup*"! Poor people cared for each other and made the best of what they had without being depressed every day. Times were tough but I don't remember any 'Food Banks' then.

Lots of people in the UK are still living in very poor conditions today which I think is a scandalous situation in this so called 'Modern Age'! At time of writing a lot of people are going to 'Food Banks' to get free food from Charities to sustain them! (*Over 900,000 people in 2013/14 in the UK*!)

The following Foodbank info from the 2014 TRUSSEL TRUST REPORT

'LATEST FOODBANK FIGURES TOP 900,000: LIFE HAS GOT WORSE NOT BETTER FOR POOREST IN 2013/14, AND THIS IS JUST THE TIP OF THE ICEBERG'

Food Banks have appeared all over Europe in the last few years. In 2012 a British Politician stated that people were only going to the Food Banks because they were there! I wonder what it's like to live in a politician's world where you only see what you want to see! They really don't have a clue as to what goes on outside of their own environment! I think a lot of them have what I call '*Ostrich Syndrome*'! Of course there are some people using Food Banks who don't really need them but as far as I know, you now have to be officially referred to them! There will always be people from all classes who will try to get something for nothing . Politicians would never do that of course just as rich people and Global Companies would never set up tax avoidance schemes! Would they?

THE LAMPLIGHTERS

The landings in the close were lit by gas lights and every night lamplighters would light them and extinguish them again in the morning. They carried a pole which had a small flame burning on the end. The pole also had a bracket fitted which was used to turn on the gas tap after which they lit the gas mantle with the flame. I think some street lamps were gas at that time also and were lit basically by the same method. I believe that after turning the street gas lights off in the morning, the lamplighters sometimes (*on request*) knocked on doors or windows with the pole to awaken people. (*The lamplighters were called 'Leeries' in some places*). The chemical carried in the lamplighters pole to fuel the flame was 'Calcium Carbide' I believe. When they emptied the Carbide, usually near a drain, we kids used to put a little water on it and watch it fizz up. I've heard that putting a drop in classmate's inkwell was great fun! Of course I would never do that!

HOME

We lived in a palatial 2 story town house in Hospital Street, the house having a front porch held up by 2 large fluted pillars and our entrance hallway had a Victorian tiled floor. A curved, carpeted staircase led up to the upper floors and we had a cook, a servant girl and a nanny to assist us in our everyday life. Our parents held many social events attended by many ladies and gentlemen in evening attire.

No, none of the above paragraph is true! I made that up! My Pinocchio nose is getting longer!!!!!

HOME ENVIRONMENT

We actually lived 2 floors up at 103 Hospital Street which was one of the 3 storey tenement buildings mentioned earlier. These tenements were built mid 1800's I believe, to house local factory and cotton mill workers, although I mostly remember shipbuilders, dockers, engineering and factory workers . The nearest cotton mills at that time that I know of were in Paisley although I know the Twomax Factory in Rutherglen Rd was a cotton mill at one time.

Our close in Hospital Street was at the junction with Cleland Street. Our house had two rooms plus a kitchen and a large box-type room behind the kitchen, big enough for a double '*built in*' bed. We also had two double beds in the smaller bedroom, one of which was a recessed bed and one bed in the large room. Our two bedroom windows overlooked Cleland Street and our kitchen window overlooked the back court, which was small as we were on the corner. We also had an indoor toilet and the toilet being inside the home was, believe it or not, a bit of a luxury as most of my friends had toilets outside on the stair landing These toilets were usually on a turn in the stairs between two floors meaning you had to walk downstairs to use the toilets! Newspaper was used as toilet paper, no toilet rolls! (*Newspaper cut to size, a hole made in the corner of the sheets, string through the hole and hung on a nail*). These outside toilets were shared by all tenants who lived on each floor, commonly three families on each landing! There were no wash basins in either the inside or outside toilets. Washing facilities in these homes were the black cast iron kitchen sink (*cold water only*) and a 'tin' (*galvanized*) bath normally kept under a bed and brought out on bath nights for the kids. Despite the absence of a bath in the house, we were all taught, and knew, how to keep ourselves clean. "*Soap and water's cheap!*" a common expression, or criticism, if people were judged to be dirty! Carbolic soap was the common soap used and is a mild disinfectant soap that contains carbolic acid, a compound that is extracted from coal tar. This soap was once the disinfectant of choice in operating rooms and private homes alike, and it still can be found in some regions of the world. There were facilities for getting a hot bath in the local Gorbals Swimming Baths. Going to 'The Baths' enabled you to get a shower and a swim. There was also a section upstairs where there were actual hot baths and you could get the use of these at a cost, towel and soap extra. Large deep baths with lashings of hot water. Great! (*Always busy on a Friday and Saturday*).

There were also local public wash-houses (*commonly known as 'Steamies'*) where housewives could go to with clothing or bedding in need of washing. A stall containing a sink could be hired and plenty of hot water and drying facilities were available. No launderettes then. An old pram was commonly used to transport the washing, washing board and soap to and from the steamie! There was an extra demand for the use of the Steamies at Christmas and New Year and consequently they were very busy. I remember in my early 'Teens' queuing all night at the steamie in Rutherglen Road to get a booking for my mother for New Year. My father brought a flask of tea in the night and came and took over in the morning. It was fun listening to the banter and occasional arguments between the women in the queue.

1885 April 17th Gorbals Baths and Wash house, 144 Main Street opened

1897 October 18th Hutchesontown Baths, 151 Rutherglen Road opened

CHRISTMAS & NEW YEAR

As you would expect Christmas presents were pretty modest in these days. On Christmas Eve we each hung a sock up on the mantlepiece above the kitchen fire and on Christmas morning we would get a few small things in the sock. This usually included a tangerine or other fruit (*which was scarce in Wartime*). There would be a few larger toys which were often handmade. My father used to make Doll's Houses with miniature furniture for the girls and wooden forts for the boys. I never found out where he kept them secretly hidden away until Christmas. There would also be a few dolls, cars and books etc.

At Christmas we looked forward to a large homemade 'Clootie (*Cloth*) Dumpling'. The cake mixture was wrapped in cloth (*sometimes a pillow case*) which was dipped in boiling water then sprinkled inside with flour. The dough was then inserted and leaving room for the mixture to expand, the cloth was tightly tied to keep it in shape, boiled for about 3 ½ hours then the dumpling removed and dried in front of the fire. A few sixpence and threepenny pieces were wrapped in greaseproof paper and placed in the mixture before cooking. I can always see in my mind's eye, a big round dumpling sitting on a rack in front of the fire, slight traces of steam rising from it, accompanied by a wonderful aroma. Delicious, and I still love
dumpling.

Homemade Ginger Wine was the drink for Christmas and New Year too. At midnight at Hogmanay (*New Year's Eve*) we could faintly here the steam ships on the Clyde sounding their foghorns to signal the New Year coming in. At this point my dad would line us up and shake our hand, wishing us a '*Happy New Year*'. He usually had a coin in his hand which was transferred to each of us when he shook our hand.

CONTINUING WITH THE HOUSES

There was one smaller block of houses on the opposite (*west*) side of Hospital Street and slightly north from us abutting Cleland Street which had bathrooms in the houses! It was a two story building which I was told belonged to 'The Railway'. Which railway company I don't know. I knew a family called Moore who lived in that building. The railway lines ran behind the houses on that side (*west side*) of

Hospital Street at a height of three stories. At home we only had gas lighting (*no electricity*) and cooking was done on the kitchen range which consisted of a coal fire which also heated the adjacent oven. (*Later we acquired a small 2 ringed gas cooker on a metal stand - no oven!*). As children we loved to toast bread by holding it with a special extendable long handled 'toasting fork' close to (*and sometimes touching*) the front bars of the fire. Delicious! The black part of the kitchen range had to be 'Black-leaded' every so often and the polished parts cleaned with an emery cloth. (*Black lead was a graphite composite I believe and emery cloth is a type of coated abrasive that has emery glued to a cloth backing; like sandpaper but much finer*).

I am indebted to my friend Danny Gill for his memories as a young boy as to how the fire in the kitchen range was lit.
"*I remember it well Alex. There was an art to lighting the fire. Getting newspaper all crunched up and building the sticks like a Red Indian Teepee but with spaces between them so that when you lit the newspaper inside you could blow air from your cheeks to help kindle the fire. Throwing a handful of sugar once it lit helped the fire on its way. Then hold a newspaper in front of the opening and you would hear the 'Whoosh' as the air drew the fire and the newspaper caught fire and disappeared up the lum* (chimney). *When the fire caught light you had previously placed wee lumps of coal on the sticks, then as the fire really caught you added more lumps of coal. Worst thing was dumping the ashes in the midden in the morning before I went to school!*"

Small bundles of firewood could be purchased in various shops, these being small sticks tied in a bundle with string but most people just gathered their own sticks. Quite a few enterprising young kids chopped up old wood and went round the doors selling bundles of firewood. Zip brand fire lighters became available in 1936. They were made up from sawdust, soaked in paraffin and bound into a block using paraffin wax. This made fire lighting much easier but of course at a cost. Handy if you were in a hurry to get the fire lit on a freezing morning!

We had a coal bunker in our lobby (h*all*). It was a deep cupboard with a shelf near the top and a board, maybe just over a foot high, on the outer edge of the bottom. The coal was emptied in there by the coal man when he made a delivery. Delivering coal to the tenements was hard work! There was no central heating, just coal fires! In later years we acquired a couple of 'Paraffin Heaters' also. As their name implies they operated by burning paraffin which we had to purchase from an Ironmonger's shop, carrying the paraffin home in a one gallon container. The only drawback with paraffin heaters is that every gallon of fuel you use puts a gallon of moisture in to the room. (*Same with bottled gas*) The amount of moisture didn't affect the old tenements but it affects modern homes!

CHIMNEY SWEEPS

As the house fires were burning coal, sooner or later a chimney sweep was required. A chimney sweep is a worker who clears ash and soot from chimneys. Chimneys may be straight or contain many changes of direction. Over a period of time, a layer of creosote can build up on the inside of the chimney which can catch fire and could potentially set the building alight. The chimney must be swept to remove the soot. This was done by a chimney sweep. In the tenements you could have a chimney stack with numerous chimney pots on it and the chimney sweep had to make sure he swept the correct one! He did this by climbing on to the roof and shouting down the chimney. When the tenant heard him and answered, he knew he had the correct chimney and could drop his weighted circular brush down. Some chimney sweeps worked from inside the house. They covered the fireplace and hearth area with cloth sheets and through a joint in the cloth. The chimney sweep working inside the room inserted a circular brush attached to a long pole and pushed this up the chimney to dislodge the soot, adding poles as required. No matter how careful they were, soot invariably escaped into the room. No fitted carpets then so not much damage, just a mess to clean!

CONTINUING WITH THE CONDITIONS

There were no 'spring interior' mattresses on the beds; mattresses were filled with clean 'Flock'. (*I believe it was called 'Rag Flock' by the manufacturers).* It was common practice to regularly empty the flock out of the mattress in to the previously mentioned empty galvanized bath and sprinkle it with 'Flea Powder' before refilling the newly laundered mattress cover! There may have been spring interior mattresses available but we didn't have them! My mother stayed at home to take care of the house and children, which was the norm in those days. The women in these days didn't have the household aids that are available nowadays. Washing clothes and bedding was all done by hand, as was mopping and sweeping floors. There were no disposable nappies! Soiled nappies had to be cleaned, washed, dried and re-used! The floors were not carpeted, only linoleum (*and rugs if you were lucky*) and any rugs were taken down to the back court, hung on a clothes rope and beaten with a carpet beater to remove any grit and dirt. (*Carpet Beaters were typically made from rattan, cane or wicker, usually interwoven into decorative but practical shapes*) Add dressing the kids, taking them to school and clinics when young, making meals, washing dishes, washing stairs, cleaning windows, ironing, sweeping and washing floors, cleaning brasses, removing the ashes from the fire and of course, shopping. You can see that a housewife's day was very busy and tiring! We did not have a 'throw away' society in these days. Torn clothes were repaired, socks with holes were darned and often boots and shoes were re-soled or re-heeled or had studs hammered on to them. Most houses had a mushroom shaped piece of wood used when darning socks. No electric irons in those days. A 'Flat Iron' was heated on the fire or gas ring and this process had to be repeated during ironing as the iron cooled down. (*Best to use TWO irons!*) Gas irons were introduced later. These had a flexible gas supply tube fitted to them and the gas actually burned inside the iron thus heating it. (*There weren't many Gas Safety regulations in those days as stringent as they are now!*) No ironing boards, the kitchen table with a folded blanket or similar on top was used. We did not have televisions, washing machines, tumble dryers, refrigerators, freezers, vacuum cleaners, electric kettles or any of the common electrical household appliances used nowadays. We did not have electricity installed in our home until after the death of my father in 1950!

We didn't have many material possessions in these days and apart from a few minor squabbles amongst siblings, life was okay. We only had a radio in the house and a 'wind -up' gramophone (*Record Player*) and some records. You had to turn a handle on the side of the gramophone to tighten the spring which turned the turntable. Board games, cards, darts, table tennis, drawing, reading and hangman were popular forms of recreation when inclement weather kept us indoors. The radio was powered by an acid type of battery and when the power ran down, we had to take the battery to a shop (*a cycle shop in Cumberland Street in our case called Kitson's*) and they took the battery to re-charge it and gave you a fully charged replacement. There was of course a charge for this service. The batteries were called 'accumulators'. My parents seemed to have enough money to 'get by' on but this changed in later years when my father's health deteriorated and then they had financial problems until his demise. No 'Social Services' giving you assistance in those days like there is today, but there was some assistance in clothing children from poor homes from the local 'Parish'. I don't know how it worked but I was the recipient of this assistance at one time. I believe my mother was given a voucher which she took to a warehouse of some kind and I received a new suit and a pair of boots. I may have got some other clothing apart from the suit etc., but I really don't remember. When you went to school you could identify everyone who had been given those suits and boots! The suits were herringbone material and all of the same colour and the boots were what we called 'Tackety boots'. As I said this assistance was from the local Parish and people knew you were 'on the Parish'. ("*Parish Suits and Tackety Boots!*" *a common expression!*)

Outdoors in the streets we played football (*watch out for the polis, I was caught twice!*), rounders, kick the can (*a form of hide & seek*) ledgy ball/dodgy ball, roller skating and we made go-carts out of old prams and orange boxes. Girls played skipping ropes, wall ball, hop scotch (*beds*) and younger kids played with 'whip and peeries' etc. (*a peerie is a small wooden spinning top that you whip to keep spinning*). If we were feeling brave and mischievous we played K.D.R.F. (*Knock door run fast!*) We were never bored when outside. Glasgow Green Park and the 'Peoples Palace' Museum and Winter Gardens' in the park were within easy walking distance and we always enjoyed going there. There were also a number of swing parks in the Gorbals. I heard that archaeologists were recently searching for old underground air raid shelters in Glasgow Green. I remember *(as a small boy)* seeing the mounds of earth on top of these shelters. It appeared as if the roofs were curved or it may just have been the mounds of earth on top. There was a number of short square brick 'chimneys or vents' protruding above the mounds in various places. A boy at school told me he had climbed down a ladder which was fixed inside the vent and saw long wooden seats along the walls inside. (He *must have had a torch with him*). Apparently no records had been kept of their whereabouts but if I remember correctly, they were near the Winter Gardens.

We didn't have much money but generally we were happy with our lot for the simple reason that we didn't know anything else! In those days any adult could chastise a child for misbehaving. If you mentioned to your parents that someone had chastised you, parents would invariably say "You must have been doing something to deserve it!" Nowadays angry parents come to your door if you chastise their children, and if you don't chastise them and they injure themselves, you'll be told you should have stopped them doing whatever it was they were doing! Can't win!

We got great enjoyment from going to the cinema when we could afford it. *(Especially the Saturday Matinee when we were young).* There was no shortage of cinemas in those days and we had about seven nearby in the Gorbals. The 'Eglinton Electreum' (*the EE's*), the Coliseum, the Bedford, the Palace, *(next to the Princess's Theatre and Diamond's Dance Academy)* the Crown Cinema (*the 'Crownie', later becoming the 'George'*) Green's Picturedrome and the Wellington Palace, which may have been in Hutchesontown, adjoining the Gorbals. There was also 'The Ritz' in Oatlands at the end of Caledonia Road. The Princess' Theatre became The Citizen's Theatre in 1945. In the Eglinton Electreum near Bridge Street Underground, the cinema was down in the basement and at times you could hear the rumble of the underground trains as they passed through the tunnels! There was also a Snooker/Billiard hall in Old Rutherglen Road just around the corner from Hospital Street called 'The Globe', but this was strictly off limits for any of us! This ruling by our parents! Snooker Halls have a much better image now than then. In those days if you could play snooker people said that was evidence of a *'miss-spent youth'!* I remember a fairly large group of men gambling in Hospital Street; between Cumberland Street and Caledonia Road. They were playing 'pitch and toss' I'm sure it was called. Betting on heads or tails landing or a combination of both as two coins were tossed into the air. A large number of people could gather at these gambling sessions. The organisers had *'cop watchers'* placed nearby at the street corners to warn them if there was any sign of police as it was obviously illegal (*as were 'back court' bookmakers at that time*). Bookmakers shops were legalised in May 1961 I think.

TRAMCARS

When we weren't walking we travelled by tramcar or underground (*called the 'Subway' in Glasgow*). The *old* tramcars had a broad coloured band painted between the lower and upper decks. They had different coloured bands for different routes. By looking at the colour you knew the tramcar's *general* route. They also had a destination board of course. If someone asked you which tram they had to take to get somewhere you could tell them to "*go across the road to the tram stop and take the "Yellow Tram*" for example. I think a Yellow Tram was a number 7 (*The number also identified the route*). The tram cars had a flight of stairs to the upper deck on both front and rear platforms. As the driver stood on the front platform, the opening to which was facing the centre of the road, you could only board or get off at the rear platform, which of course faced the pavement. Trams were powered by electricity and ran on rails. The electricity was supplied by overhead wires and an apparatus called a 'Pantograph' was attached to the roof of the tram and this conducted the current from the single wire to the tram. The return current was earthed through the tram's steel wheels and rail tracks. New trams were eventually introduced (*Coronation type I think they were called*) on which the driver sat in isolation in a little cabin, one at each end of the tram. Trams did not turn around to make the return journey. The drivers simply carried the required hand controls from one cabin to the other to make the return journey. In other words what was the back became the front! All the double seats faced forward in the direction of travel and so, for the return journey, the conductor had to walk along between the seats pulling the backs of the seats (*which were hinged*) forward so that the new passengers were facing the direction of travel again. He also had to adjust the position of the Pantograph making it slope to the rear of the tram and he did this by pulling on a rope which was attached to it. Simple system but effective! With the exception of emergencies, all repairs to the tram tracks and surrounding cobblestones (*which were the norm*) were carried out during the night. The workmen, tools and materials were transported to the area by a tramcar which was made for this purpose. If I remember correctly it was about half the height of normal tramcars which were double decked. In April 1949 Glasgow Corporation Transport started to replace the trams with 'Trolleybuses' which also used overhead wires (*two wires*) to power them but did not require rails. They were much quieter than tramcars and you had to ensure that you checked that there were none in the vicinity before crossing the road! The trolleybuses had two spring loaded poles to transfer power from two overhead wires to the bus. One positive and one negative to complete the circuit. The last Glasgow tram ran on September 1962. The last trolleybuses ran in May 1967 and were replaced by Leyland 'Atlantean' diesel buses. At one time when I was about twelve, I decided I would try to 'dodge' paying my fare on a tramcar. I was upstairs and when the conductor came upstairs to collect the fares, I stared out of the window and pretended not to hear him! The conductor tapped me on the shoulder and despite my protestations of innocence, ("*I was deep in thought!*") gave me a telling off in front of the rest of the passengers and collected the fare! I expect he had plenty of previous experience with fare dodgers! Of course at the time I didn't realise that if a Ticket Inspector came on, the conductor could be in trouble! I bet my face was red!

This also reminded me of the time that one of my neighbours from the 1st floor in our close and myself, decided to 'bunk off' school. We made our way to the Fruit Market which was near the city centre at that time and was a place of real hustle and bustle, with horses and carts, busy porters and dealers calling out prices. We had only been there about half an hour when I heard a well known voice from above my head ask, "*What are you doing here?*" It was my father at the top of a ladder and he was doing a bit of sign-writing or painting on the front of the building! I never tried to dodge paying my fare or bunk off school again!

I don't remember a great deal of my very young childhood but I remember I had my tonsils removed in the Victoria Infirmary. I remember walking along a corridor holding a nurse's hand and she was telling me we were going to the theatre, "*To see Mickey Mouse*" she said! I remember waking up lying on a large waterproof cover on the floor. There were other children beside me, some of whom were being sick, and that's all I remember about it and because our throats were rather raw after the operation we were given ice-cream.

I also remember an unpleasant and very painful incident at home involving myself and a clothes wringer. My mother had fitted the wringer to the kitchen table and was putting wet washing through the wringer to remove as much water as possible from the clothes. The bottom roller on the wringer was operated by turning a handle fitted to the end of the roller and this roller, by means of cog wheels, turned the upper roller in the opposite direction. I'm guessing I was about three or four years old and was watching my mother working at the table. I was at the side of the wringer watching the cogs meshing together and whether by accident or deliberate action on my part, my second finger on my right hand got caught in the meshing cogs and they took the top off my finger! The Ringer won that round! (*Later models of wringer had a guard over the cogs*).

In view of the previous three paragraphs, does anyone know where I can get some 'Lucky White Heather'?

I don't know where my father was at this point but I remember him taking me by Tramcar to the Glasgow Royal Infirmary where my finger got the treatment required. I also remember that on the tram some sympathetic adults gave me small amounts of money. From then my life was as any normal child in these days, playing various games with friends on the streets and back courts, going to primary school etc. etc.

SCHOOL

I went to primary school about 1938, the school being Camden Street School, a small local school with at least one 'claim to fame', an MP

had been educated there, his name was George Buchanan. He was MP for the Gorbals from 1922 to 1948. In 1945 he was made 'Under-Secretary of State for Scotland' and was made UK 'Minister for Pensions' in 1947. He was sworn to the 'Privy Council' in 1948. Not bad for a Gorbals boy!
(*The Privy Council is a formal body of advisors to the Sovereign in the UK*)

Strangely enough I don't remember much details of my education in Camden St school other than it was okay. I remember a newsagents shop (*I think*) in Caledonia Road, just round the corner from Camden Street school that had an arcade machine on the wall into which you put one penny to operate. You then grasped two brass handles like door knobs (*one of which turned*) and an electric current passed through your body! The more you turned the handle the greater the surge of electricity. Two or three persons could hold hands and the current passed through all of these persons! I believe these machines were battery operated, which is just as well! After Camden Street school I went to Adelphi Terrace School until I was 15. We walked to and from school in these days as they were in the locality.

SHOPPING

In the 1930's and 1940's there were no supermarkets. There was no sliced bread and bread was not wrapped as it is now. There was no pre-packed food as we see now. Cheese for example was displayed in the shop as a large portion and you indicated to the shop assistant the size of portion you required. The assistant then cut the required portion, weighed it and charged you accordingly. Butter could also be purchased in the same manner. When rationing was introduced during WW2 the portion sizes were limited by weight of course. Children had their own ration books which were more generous than those of adults. Pre-school children had allowances of cod-liver oil and orange juice. The concentrated orange juice was okay (*I personally liked it*) but the cod-liver oil was horrible and many children wouldn't take it so it became available as 'cod liver oil and malt'. This was a thick brown substance with the consistency I would say of honey and tasted fine. It had to be spooned out of a large jar and lots of kids really liked it. We did our shopping in local shops. Butchers,

Bakers, Dairies, Grocers, Fruit Shops, Greengrocers, Fishmongers, Shoe Shops, Clothes Shops, Shoe Repairers, Cycle Shops, Haberdasheries, Newsagents and Kosher Butchers for the Jewish community etc. were all in the neighbourhood or adjoining districts.

If I remember correctly, Cumberland Street was one of the best streets for shopping. It was a long street and it had a great variety of shops and was always very busy. When there was a heavy fall of snow shopkeepers cleared snow from pavements along the whole front of their shops using shovels, or if icy, sprinkling salt. This meant that in busy streets with lots of shops long lengths of pavement were cleared for pedestrians. There were no plastic bags. Your items were put into a paper bag where applicable. Other items were put directly into your shopping bag or basket. There was no 'self-service' and there were no calculators! You asked the shop assistant for an item and the assistant wrote down the price of each item as they were given to you then totalled the prices up and charged you accordingly. With the exception of tinned food there was no 'Pre-packed' food or 'Ready Meals', only the ingredients to enable you to prepare and cook your own meals. Tea was made in a teapot using loose tea leafs; there were no 'tea bags'. I also remember bottles of 'Camp Coffee'. (*Coffee & Chicory, which I think is still available*).
There were no 'fast food' outlets except 'fish and chip' shops and some cafés who provided a snack. I remember my father and mother making jam and marmalade in a large copper jelly pan at home.

Wrapping - Goods were wrapped in brown paper which was the common wrapping medium at the time. When purchasing clothes for example, the clothes were loosely folded (*so as not to crush them*) and wrapped in brown paper then tied with string. Most homes had some brown paper and string in a drawer. Brown paper was also used to cover school books! I remember my father wrapping parcels with brown paper, tying them with string then applying sealing wax to the knots to secure the parcel. Wax was sometimes used to secure the flap on an envelope if it contained something of importance. There was also a type of waterproof brown paper available if my memory serves me right. It was brown on one side and black, like thin tar, on the other. This was useful for lining interwoven wicker hampers for example, which were commonly used in those days.

Carts - I remember a person coming round our local streets with a small hand cart selling milk, buttermilk and also cream I think. You took a large jug down to the cart and the jug was filled with one of the above. I can't remember what that cost but I remember taking a jug down to get buttermilk for my father. It wasn't a flat handcart. It had a box type curved roof structure which contained urns and some measuring cups hanging from hooks. There were no ice-cream vans. Flat handcarts were common then and could be hired locally. (*Usually from 'Hyslop' whose premises were in a lane just off Cleland St. The lane may have been the back entrance*). When people moved house in these days they usually only moved a few streets away and hired these carts to carry their few belongings, making the number of trips required.

CURRENCY

Our currency was different then. We used pounds, shillings and pence. 12 pence in a shilling and 20 shillings in a pound making 240 pence in a pound. We had farthing coins - one quarter of a pence and half-penny coins. We also had 3 pence and 6 pence coins, a 1 shilling coin, a 2 shilling coin and a half-crown coin (*worth 2 shillings and 6 pence*). We had £5 notes, £1 notes and 10 shilling notes. Currency calculations were therefore a bit more difficult then. Decimal currency as used today was introduced in February 1971.

Note - Old penny coins are still used to adjust the weights that control the time on the Great Clock in the Elizabeth Tower in London, commonly known as 'Big Ben'. Big Ben is actually the clock bell. (*The tower was renamed The Elizabeth Tower in 2012 in honour of Queen Elizabeth II's Diamond Jubilee*)

LINEAR MEASURE

The Linear Measure used then was yards, feet and inches not metres and centimetres. The UK joined the EEC in 1973 and were obliged under the Treaty to adopt Metrication within 5 years. You can see the old Standard Measures in stone on the front south corner of the

Glasgow City Chambers building in George Square. (*The corner facing the Square*). I remember seeing it when I was young.

RECYCLING

There was no recycling as we recognise it now but empty milk bottles were returned to the dairy or milkman for re-use. Beer bottles and soft drink bottles like lemonade for example, were also returned to shops and you got a small amount of cash back on each bottle. These were the children's favourite and some weans worked hard to collect empty bottles. I've heard that at one time this refund system was also used with glass jam jars.

THE NHS (National Health Service)

There was no National Health Service. The NHS didn't come in to being until 5th July 1948. If you required medical help, treatment or prescription, you had to pay for it! If you needed to visit a doctor, or have him come to your home, you had to pay for it! When you took your prescription to the Chemist you had to pay for it! You didn't make an appointment with the doctor, you had to go to the surgery and wait your turn to see him. Our family doctor was Dr Percival Baird and his surgery was in Crown Street which was near our home. (2 *streets away*). He was a brilliant man who had an amazing memory for the names and addresses of his patients *and* their previous ailments. (*and he didn't charge too much*)! Due to the overcrowding, as mentioned earlier, infectious illness and diseases spread quickly. Most children were born at home in those days and all the experienced female neighbours helped with the birth. A lot of them had large families themselves, hence the experience. All of my family and friends were born at home. Lots of children died very young. One of the first things many people did (*if they could afford it*) was take out an insurance policy. Usually a 'One Penny Policy' for very young children.

Most people did not have telephones (*I didn't know of any*) and in an emergency had to use telephone boxes or a friendly shopkeeper. The other alternative was to use the 'Police Boxes' which were strategically positioned in large numbers throughout the city. (*A vast network of 323 boxes at one time in Glasgow*). These were originally coloured Red in Glasgow because they were maintained by the Post Office but were changed to Blue in the late 1960's. They looked a bit like the one in the 'Doctor Who' TV series but I think they looked a little bit different inside! The police constables used these boxes to telephone their Station and when the Station wanted to contact the constables, the blue light on the top flashed on and off. The boxes had a small door on the outside which covered a mesh type grill. The public could open the door and by talking into the mesh, communicate with a Police Office via a speakerphone. I'm also pretty sure I saw a '*break the glass*' fire alarm on the outside of a building in Crown Street at the junction with Old Rutherglen Road. I think it was a Bank Of Scotland building. The public could use these to raise the alarm if there was a fire in the vicinity.

APPENDIX

My older brother told me that my father was part on a three man Vickers Machine Gun team in WW1 but I thought he was a baker! I'm sure he told me he went in to France with all 'buns glazing!' (*Sorry about that; couldn't resist it!*)

OVERCROWDING

In the 1930's the population of Glasgow was more densely packed than any other city in Europe, one of the reasons being an expansion of industry which attracted immigrants from Ireland and the Highlands. Plans had been in place I believe since the 1930's to ease this but with the exception of Pollok, which was started pre-war and finished in 1951, the other three large peripheral housing estates did not start until the 1950's these being:-

1. Drumchapel in 1951;
2. Castlemilk in 1954; and
3. Easterhouse in 1955.

Each was designed to accommodate 50,000 people.

OVERSPILL

Glasgow Council also had an 'overspill' plan and people were moved away from Glasgow to designated areas outside the city. Cumbernauld was designated a new town and was built in 1955. Other areas were East Kilbride, Irvine, Glenrothes and Livingston.

Sweet rationing ended in February 1953, and sugar rationing ended in September of that year.

The final end of all rationing did not come until 1954 with the end of it on meat and bacon.

Rationing stopped on the 4th July 1954.

CHAPTER 5

Windae Hingin

Remember the Gorbals of years ago, and my memory I do dredge,
I kin see my Ma and my Granny, all leaning on their windae ledge.

Soo-siders caw it windaw hingin, speakin to neighbours next door,
With a pillow or cushion under their elbows, as they cood get sore.

Chattin to your pals either side, ye'd hear aw aboot peoples capers,
The news got passed by word of mouth, who needed newspapers?

Always lookin outside yer kitchen windae, doin your windae hingin,
No doin it fae the back windae the smell o the middens were mingin.

Watching the drunks coming oot of the pubs, it held us all in a trance,
With a fish supper in their pocket, as they sang and gave ye a dance.

Then a wummin from across the street, started making a big racket,
Aw naw that's my man, I hope he hizny spent all of his wage packet.

The tenements got demolished, replaced wae buildings quite dreamy,
And windae hingin's a thing of the past, just like gaun tae the steamie.

The Pictures

Before the TV, videos and facebook took all of our lives over,
Gaun to the picture hoose wiz like finding a four leaf clover.

You'd pay fur your tickets for the balcony or maybe the stalls,
There wiz so many picture hooses covering the auld Gorbals.

The usherette now shone her torch, for all of us to find a seat,
Cos' if she diddny it was so dark, you might trip over yer feet.

The movies cood show James Cagney or the lovely Doris Day,
Interval time the lassie wood came roon wae the ice cream tray.

The back row was for winchers aw cuddling and a bit o kissing,
And never cared about the film that both of them were missing.

Saturday morning matinees had films fur the weans oh so funny,
Their Ma's had given them the entrance fee with pocket money.

But now I'm an auld pensioner my diary hasn't so many fixtures,
I remember with great pleasure oor night oot at the local pictures.

The Dampies

The architects must have been bampots and builders namby pambys,
To design all those buildings, that Gorbals people called the Dampies.

The tenements were demolished, for new houses so brave and bold,
But these dwellings wur full of dampness wae green and black mould.

Families with weans became very ill, these houses were a big disaster,
With fungus growing wild and wallpaper peelin aff soaking wet plaster.

Glasgow District Council said, we know of a way to get rid of this damp,
Just keep your windaes wide open and all your heaters on at full ramp.

But the residents said enough's enough an a rent strike did commence,
Until it wiz agreed that they'd be demolished, now that did make sense.

So with the Dampies days now numbered, they will never be forgotten,
With condensation an' breathing problems, these buildings were rotten.

And now ends my saga of the Dampies thank God they'll soon be dead,
As people aw raise a glass in cheer in the nearby pub The Brazen head.

Housing Schemes and Broken Dreams

At the time of the Gorbals clearance we were shifted to houses new,
As the clearance started we got told houses for all, not jist for a few.

To Castlemilk/Toryglen and other places, we were told wur sublime,
With us having an inside toilet and a bath for the very very first time.

Most of us punters if given the choice, said we jist diddny want to go,
Half demolished tenements that once had warm fires no longer glow.

Sure at first it was exciting to meet new pals in the housing schemes,
But when the novelty wore aff it wiz a case of soo-side broken dreams.

Cos' back in the soo-side we'd picture hooses, pubs an shops galore,
And we coodny wait to get a bus back, to the place that we did adore.

Nae shops or amenities planned, planners lacked so much inspiration,
The very same thing happened next door in the Oatlands regeneration.

There's new houses built all over the soo side or so it somehow seems,
But the soo-side of my era will last on forever an ever in all my dreams.

Saltcoats By The Sea

For two weeks in the summer, we had a holiday feeling so rare,
Cos most people in the soo side went away fur the Glesga Fair.

Ma and Da took oor family oan the bus oer tae the Central Station,
I was burstin with excitement 'cause Saltcoats wiz oor destination.

We stayed in a boarding house just five minutes walk fae the sea,
There wiz Ma and Da, my big sister, and my wee granny and me.

Every day wiz a beach day Ma, Da and Granny would sit an natter,
Grandas with rolled up trooser legs, wid paddle in the sea watter.

Breathing in that salt sea air every day, it was for us a magic treat,
Wizzny half a big change fae Caledonia Rd or Cumberland Street.

During the day a big ice cream, and at night-times a poke of chips,
Even jist thinking about it nowadays still has me smacking my lips.

But soon oor holiday was over and it was goodbye from you n me,
I coodny wait to tell my soo side pal's, aboot Saltcoats by the sea.

Gaun Back In Time

I write this poem from my memory, so it's written with no disdain,
To a time when oor life's wiz magic and you and I were a wean.

Dreepin aff dyke's, playing kick the can, or aff rakin the midges,
When parents didn't have TV sets or these super duper fridges.

The lassies playing skippin ropes, oor streets held nae dangers,
Boys aw playing fitbaw dreaming of playing fur Celtic or Rangers.

Hard to believe that in those far off days, we diddny have telly's,
We were just contented splashin in puddles in oor trusted wellies.

Then you heard a bugle being blown, us wean's would all swoon,
T'was the Rag and Bone man, fur old claes we'd all get a balloon.

Pubs on every corner, yer messages oan the tic, we hiddny a care,
Your Ma would never dream of missing her turn of washin the stair.

This happened to me over sixty years ago as I pen my wee rhyme,
I'm jist a proud auld soo-side pensioner, who is gaun back in time.

Stairheid Toilet

Can you remember years ago when the old tenements were standing,
To go to the toilet you'd hiv to walk downstairs to the stairheid landing.

There were three families who would share oor toilet, as off you'd go,
But if there wiz an emergency, then under the bed we kept the old po.

You'd try and announce your presence, by whistling like a wee budgie,
And if you heard a cough then you knew somebody wiz in the cludgie.

Waiting your turn to go to the stairheid toilet really wiz a common thing,
And you prayed that there wiz newspaper hingin fae that bit of o string.

Winter times cood be dark so you took a lit candle, naw ye wurrny vain,
Then run like mad back up the stairs after you'd pulled the lavvy chain.

Then oor tenements got demolished we got moved to housin schemes,
We had a bath and an inside toilet, it was the answer to all oor dreams.

But I'll never forget the stairheid toilet for as long as my old heart beats,
As we repose in our luxury en-suite bathrooms, with heated toilet seats.

Fish and Chips

Today you can have an Indian or Chinese food in a silver foiled- tray,
When I was a wean the Fish n Chip shop wiz oor fast food take away.

A special Fish Supper wrapped up in newspaper, made us aw swoon,
Wae a bottle of Irn Bru or American Cream Soda tae wash it aw doon.

Now some people in the soo side would say Anns Fry passed the test,
But we all have different opinions, of what Fish n Chip shop wiz best.

Aye some say it wiz Mario's but it wiz really hard for all of us to decide,
So who knows what the best Fish n Chip shop was in aw the soo-side.

Friday night wiz the main night of the week fur all us Fish n Chip eaters,
And there used to be a mile long queue outside of auld Greasy Peter's.

And who remembers those battered fritters, oh they really did hit the mark,
People fae Oatlands used Giovannis chipper opposite of Richmond Park.

I don't like the home delivery of Curry's/Pizzas to tell ye the honest truth,
I'd rather be queuing ootside o the Fish n Chip shop slaverin at the mooth.

The Coalman

From the far off end of Oatlands, all the way over up to Eginton Toll,
Came Jackson's Coal Merchant's lorry,with hunner's a bags of coal.

From your Tenement windae lookin below, the coalman wiz standing,
You'd shout down two bags fur Mrs Wilson up on the second landing.

Opening the wooden bunker in your lobby, closing the doors a must,
Cos' when the coal wiz dumped ye coodny see fur aw the bloody dust.

The coalman stood there in your lobby black with coal fae head to toe,
After paying him he'd rejoin his lorry, and off to the next street he'd go.

Jackson's used to have horses and carts before lorries joined his fleet,
The horses were kept in the Pen in between Sandyfaulds and Moffat St.

Also in the soo side you had no chance of missin Jackson's coal patrol,
Cos' the guy on the back of the lorry, burst his lungs shouting "Cahole".

Jacksons Coal Merchants are in the past, their coal we no longer desire,
Nowadays we have central heating or a new thing called an electric fire.

Gorbals Cross

When I think of the Gorbals clearance, it leaves me at a loss,
Not only were the houses demolished but also Gorbals Cross.

Traffic was always busy, all along Norfolk and Ballater Street,
Shops were everywhere, goin fur the messages wiz a treat.

Up Gorbals St you had the baths where we'd all go for a swim,
Then after go to the Hot Peanut man, didn't us weans love him.

Round Gorbals Cross you had oh so many pubs, to enjoy a jar,
Too many pubs to name so I'll jist say Doyle's and Benny's Bar.

Then stood the Citizens Theatre, the Palace Cinema next door,
With the Princess Cafe and chip shops, ye coodny ask fur more.

But as I say this has all gone now, no more are people meeting,
And after being away over 45 years I looked and felt like greetin.

In progress's name Gorbals Cross was destroyed, whit a shame,
For with its destruction, oor generation will never feel the same.

Queen o' the Steamie

She was known as Queen o' the Steamie, her name Agnes McSweeney,
Filling her pram up wae washing, shirts, skirts and a dirty auld peeney.

Livin in an old Tenement hoose two stairs up in busy Cumberland Street,
Always first to finish her washing, oor Agnes she wiz never wance beat.

Before she left the Steamie, she wid share the gossip wae other maws,
Did ye hear aboot oor big Ella living in sin oot by in sunny Pollokshaws.

Or what aboot free and easy Isa, who's new baby she's called it Davie,
How can that be her man's been away fur 2 years in the Merchant Navy.

So Agnes done it once again left aw the other washin wummen standing,
That's it fur another week, as she pushed her pram up onta her landing.

She went back in her hoose, resting her feet while drinking a cup of tea,
Thinking because I left the Steamie early, are they gossiping aboot me.

This was a century ago now, kitchens hiv washing machines so dreamy,
It's a long time now since Agnes McSweeney was Queen o' the Steamie.

The Fair Fortnight

For the last two weeks in July, most of Glasgow folk said goodbye,
Going away fur the Fair and hoping that the weather would be dry.

Lots of Gorbals people went to Rothesey or Dunoon wae a big smile,
While others went to Blackpool for two weeks along its Golden mile.

Everyone seemed to be so happy, we had money and it wiz the Fair,
Ye cood go to Billy Butlins holiday camp just opened up doon in Ayr.

My Ma and Da took us tae Saltcoats, we travelled there by the train,
Then a new thing called a package holiday took folks over to Spain.

Changing your money to pesetas aff to Espana withoot even a ruffle,
Where you drank San Miguel aw night and done the soo side shuffle.

Oh life wiz great fun fur the Fair fortnight, suntanned as dark as hide,
But all too soon it wiz over as we all travelled back to the old soo side.

Back to the auld Sunny Gorbals, by boat, car, train or even the plane,
We knew we were aw back hame because it wiz lashin doon wae rain.

Black and White TV Set
==

When Ma and Da got our first TV set there was no salesman flannel,
How cood there be when the telly only had the one bloomin channel.

Taking the 101 Trolley bus along to Crown St and Stirling Hunters shop,
Right beside the Wheatsheaf Pub where ye had a pint and a wee drop.

Now this was the early Fifties and TV sets were just new on the scene,
And all oor neighbours chapped on oor door, jist to look at the screen.

BBC wiz the only channel, programmes ended jist after eleven at night,
Unless it wiz Hogmanay and we got an hour's extra view after midnight.

We got a bonus with the new ITV channel and thought we're in heaven,
Never ever thinking that in years to come we'd watch television for 24/7.

Neighbours came to watch oor TV set, Saturday night wiz like ra pictures,
When ITV adverts came on we'd aw pass round a plate of Dolly Mixtures.

Black and White TV sets go back to the days we were seen but no heard,
Other countries take note it wiz invented by Scotsman, John Logie Baird.

Wedding Scramble

I think of an event years ago, and I explain it without any preamble,
As adults and weans alike, got ready for the Weddin day scramble.

Bride and Groom jist newly married looked oh so happy and sweet,
And covered in confetti they went intae the Weddin car's back seat.

Then as the car's moved away, the Groom's window it wound down,
And from his hand leaped a mixture of coins to land on the ground.

Then all Hell broke loose as the coins were thrown, oh what a scatter,
Men, women and weans dived in to the scramble, age diddny matter.

Pushin and shoving with elbows used, to try and get a penny or two,
Somebody got a broken finger and some poor wee soul lost a shoe.

The lucky wans who'd grabbed a penny went to spend it in the shop,
The unlucky wans looked a mess, the wean wae nae shoe did a hop.

Yes getting married then having a family, it is all part of life's gamble,
But not as much as diving in head first at the Wedding day scramble.

The Jeely Piece

My favourite sandwich in all the World, I honestly mean this really,
It is in between two slices of breid with a great big dollop of Jeely.

As weans playing in the back courts amongst middens so smelly,
You could sometimes get a hungry feeling in the pit of your belly.

Shouting up to your Ma's windae hoping she wizzny oe'r the Toon,
Aw Ma ah'm bloomin starving gonny throw me a Jeely piece doon.

Then your Ma's windae, rolled up, oh it was a sound so very sweet,
And your Jeely piece wrapped up in bread paper landed at yer feet.

You scooped up your piece just as soon as it landed on the ground,
But shared it with some of your china's as they gathered all around.

This was us all years ago as weans dirty but happy caked in grime,
As we reminisce back fondly on the auld Gorbals once upon a time.

So forget about your bacon rolls or breakfasts swimming in grease,
Cause there's nothing in this wide World that kin beat a Jeely piece.

Soo Side Forever

Where do I begin to tell ye a tale that will make you want to sigh,
It's about an area of Glesga where a lifetime ago I said goodbye.

Passin Oatlands to Hutchesontown, Gorbals, Laurieston wae pride,
This is where we were born in Glasgow's world famous soo side.

We aw knew each other and in oor streets, there wiz no strangers,
Some supported Clyde FC as others supported Celtic or Rangers.

Oor community spirit was legendary till the tenements came down,
Then we all moved out to housing schemes outside Glasgow Town.

Some others like Shuggy Burns fled to Oz thousands a miles away,
Or like Marjorie Quills who moved to Florida in the good old U.S.A.

The tenements have long gone now and oor community spirit taken,
But oor memories will always remain there they'll never be forsaken.

See you can never erase a memory as we carry on with endeavour,
Hogmanay time we raise oor glasses, it's the soo side, aye forever.

Gorbals Columbo

Hollywood has all of it's film stars, or actors in many a TV show,
But we have a superstar and it's oor own Gorbals dug Columbo.

You will see him in the soo side, walked by our own Lynne Lees,
And when the Lady dogs see him they all go weak at the knees.

Gary Moore also takes him for walks Columbos King o the mutts,
While his favourite pastime is sniffin oot those hidden doughnuts.

Everyone loves Columbo, soo siders think he's definitly the most,
Lynne posted a video of him barking at the Brazen Heads ghost.

He's a dedicated follower of fashion, he'll never look like a wreck,
Lynne dresses him up as a cowboy, with a bandana on his neck.

Such a character with those very sad eyes we all love him to bits,
And those extra wide ears pick up as he hears the word biscuits.

Aye Columbo used to be in the Cumbie we know he's not a mug,
Every year he wins the best prize fur Gorbals best dressed dug.

The Shows

Who remembers years ago when we were young and life so serene,
And every summer we went to the Shows jist over in Glasgow green.

The Wurlitzer spun roon so fast and the Ghost train made ye scream,
Weans were eatin toffee apples or candy floss to them it wiz a dream.

Pop music was in the air, as people all gathered there in their throngs,
Some gangs would have a fight, Cumbie, Derry or the Calton Tongs.

Yer Ma and Granny would play Housey Housey hopin they would win,
Fortune telling by Madame Za Za but it cost a shilling for you to go in.

Stall owners shouting out come try yer luck and win a coconut or two,
But I never saw anyone win one they must have been stuck wae glue.

See this is the Shows that I used to know when I wiz a soo side wean,
Dive Bombers and the big Dipper so fast but I'll never see them again.

Because I left old Glesga Toon about a life time ago as the story goes,
But in my mind I'll always be a soo side wean gaun over to the Shows.

The First Gorbals Reunion (Part 1)

I caught the early morning Virgin train, which left Euston railway station,
Heading back to Glasgow Town the Gorbals reunion wiz my destination.

On Friday the 8th of August we gathered in the Glencairn club en masse,
And fair play to Christina Gray for all her planning it was really first class.

People from all over the Gorbals entered aw the doors fae seven o'clock,
When the time reached nine o'clock the Glencairn was really choc a bloc.

Gorbals folks do have a heart of Gold not often that they make any rickets,
With special thanks going out to Gerry Gracie, for selling the raffle tickets.

Folks aw sat down having a drink or two talking about Gorbals of the past,
What a great turn out on the night the Gorbals reunion it really wiz a blast.

The bar staff kept us supplied in drink all night, working so busily at full tilt,
And Lynne Lees even brought along Gorbals Columbo dressed up in a kilt.

Steve Birrell started up the Old Gorbals Pictures and what a wonderful site,
With Christina Gray as admin while organising such a truly wonderful night.

The First Gorbals Reunion (Part 2)

And to London I now headed back, Glasgow's so many miles away,
But the Gorbals Reunion Night will be talked about for many's a day.

The buzz of aw the folk in the Glencairn, the peel of all their laughter,
With a mighty cheer for St Francis Pipe Band it lifted the roofs rafter.

All those gorgeous Gorbals burds, beautiful as any film star can be,
And me sitting lookin at them wishing once again I was twenty three.

Then we had the raffle ticket draws, so many prizes for your delight,
Wae the Hospice getting two thousand pound collected on the night.

Everybody was taking photos, images preserved for the future to see,
The Glencairn Club held the Gorbals Reunion, this wiz the place to be.

People were all up dancing, who cared if your clothes got a wee ruffle,
The dance floor was crowded, you could only dae the soo side shuffle.

So the Gorbals Reunion at the Glencairn was a night beyond compare,
We're all in the Gorbals History book now, for you and I were all there.

Spinning the Bottle

Today we all have Hi Fi system's to hear our music at full throttle,
But the tenements had few record players, we'd jist spin the bottle.

The pubs all closed at 10 o'clock pm but we were never at a loose,
'Cause we'd buy a kerry oot and have a party in someone's hoose.

The drink was poured the glasses filled, as we quenched oor thirst,
Then we would spin the bottle to see who would be up singing first.

The bottle stopped spinning, it's neck pointed at first to sing a song,
Giving it laldy the singer sang out in a voice shaky but quite strong.

Everybody took their turn and sang quickly or maybe smoochy slow,
Even if the guy was knocking the ceiling from his hoose doon below.

We were all enjoying ourselves but the kerry oot diddny last too long,
With oor appointed M.C. on the night shouting "wan singer wan song."

Aye we aw knew how to party in the tenement's of the Gorbals past,
As we all dutifully spun the bottle belting oot our song's at full blast.

Cumberland Street

The toon had Argyle and Sauchiehall Street to buy yourself a treat,
But nothing could compare with all the shops in Cumberland Street.

You had Saint Francis' Chapel with the Paragon Cinema next door,
A flea ridden picture hoose aw the hard benches made yer bum sore.

Butchers, bakers and linen shops, can't really name a shop not there,
The Barbers where a bowl got stuck on mah heid, as he cut my hair.

Passing by Lawmoor St Police Station, the polis were all tough cops,
But never gave it a second glance as we looked in all of those shops.

A pub was on every corner fur a man to drink a pint and a wee dram,
Women were oot for the messages while pushin her wean in a pram.

I'll never forget all of those shops, walking wae my Ma and my Granny,
As they tried to spot a bargain, us soo-siders were known to be canny.

These Gorbals shops were better than Sauchiehall St in my estimation,
Sadly they are a thing of the past, jist like Cumberland St railway station.

Shawfield Stadium

Fun years ago was watchin Sunday night at the London Palladium,
But Greyhound punters all headed for a bet at Shawfield Stadium.

They went on a Tuesday or Friday night, wae money in their pocket,
Praying out, very loudly their dog would run like a supersonic rocket.

Most punters lost cash as their Greyhounds were slow out the stalls,
And didn't have their fare home so it wiz a walk back to the Gorbals.

Also years ago at Shawfield ye had a football team called Clyde FC,
But to the support who went to watch them they were the Bully Wee.

A great wee team they were, but now they hiv changed their ground,
Hoping fur better days and praying fame and fortune cood be found.

Beside dugs and fitba, you'd speedway racing, and a hall fur a dance,
A guy winning money on Friday night's dugs had money for romance.

But Greyhound punters are happy people their misery is only fleeting,
Cos if they lost on Tuesday they were sure to win at the next meeting.

Friday Night Bath

Who remembers getting washed in the sink or the old tin bath,
At the time I felt like greetin but as I look back now I can laugh.

I'd so dread Friday nights and the sound of the whistling kettle,
Cause with it's boiling water Ma would fill up this bath of metal.

The auldest wean went in first like they were King o the Castle,
The youngest had to wait their turn saying I hate all this hassle.

Well your Ma scrubbed you so hard that your skin it turned Rid,
People of my generation know this is the truth I sure do not kid.

Drying yourself in front of the open fire feeling so clean n sleek,
Listening to your siblings saying but Ma I had a bath last week.

But as you grow aulder you're life can change to being dreamy,
Cos yer Ma gave ye money for a hot bath in the local Steamie.

And now I have a bathroom so big it would give you a real fright,
I think back tae the soo side and that tin bath every Friday night.

The Albert Bridge

How many times have you crossed over it, by bus, car or walking,
But the state of the Albert Bridge today I'm afraid it is so shocking.

Like all bridges spanning the Clyde we proudly know their names,
The Albert got a pink sheet cover fur the Commonwealth games.

One end o the bridge is Saltmarket headin to the Toon big n wide,
The other end is Crown St once full of shops for us in the soo side.

The Albert displays Glasgow's Coat of Arms to us it is so entrusted,
Though sadly the weather over the years has left this motto rusted.

There's many a bridge built over the Clyde for its people, you n me,
As this mighty river passes Govan shipyards on it's way to the sea.

What can be done to repair the Albert back to its once former glory,
We must all get active to highlight its plight and highlight this story.

People have founded a new campaign it's growing bigger every day,
Refurbish the Albert back to its former glory that's what the folk say.

The White Lady

The Southern Necropolis holds many graves beneath trees so shady,
But the monument that holds us all in awe is that of the "White Lady".

Here lays John S Smith, his wife Magdalene and housekeeper Mary,
When you hear about this legend, it is both poignant and also scary.

Both of the ladies got killed by a tram on a wet dark Glasgow day,
So John S Smith erected this monument so their memory will stay.

This White Lady monument stands alone and has a story of its own,
Cause if you look at her and she turns her head, you'll turn to stone.

If you shout 'White Lady White Lady' run round her three times fast,
The graveyard legend says you'll be ok into stone you won't be cast.

Southern Necropolis has many people of stature all laying now at rest,
Be it Sir Thomas Lipton, or whoever, but I like the White Lady the best.

This was the legend of the White Lady and hope ye enjoyed the story,
May God look over all in the Southern Necropolis as they lay in Glory.

Oatlands Dream

Last night I had a dream as I took a trip down memory lane,
And found myself in the Oatlands where once I was a wean.

Oor tenements were still standing, no they hadn't gone at all,
Lassies were busy playing peever boys aw kicking a football.

At Richmond Park feeding swans was great for you and me,
Then walking along Rutherglen Rd, to spit at the Devil's tree.

In the morning out to school WolseleySt or Bonnie's we'd go,
The future would change Big Bonnies to name it John Bosco.

Getting older we'd visit the pubs if we were feeling at a loose,
Used to do oor back seat winching in the Ritz Picture Hoose.

Those were the days, we were young and as happy as a lark,
With your Da you'd watch Clyde FC over by at Shawfield Park.

When I woke this morning my Oatlands dream had took flight,
No need to worry I'm dreaming about Oatlands again tonight.

The Pawn Shop

In the tenements of old with oor people living on the edge,
The pawn shop was our saviour with your articles to pledge.

Nobody liked to be spotted going in, it did take a bit of nerve,
If you saw a neighbour, you'd give them the old body swerve.

The one I remember was John the Pawn in Braehead Street,
At the junction where Cally and Rutherglen Roads did meet.

Each Monday morning my Da's suit was pledged so it seemed,
But come Friday morning my Ma went back to get it redeemed.

Cash was tight and our Mothers would give each other a haun,
Although as a last resort they really thanked God fur the Pawn.

My generation remember the pawn though some say it's a fable,
But if it wizzny for oor Uncle there would be no food on the table.

So now my wee poem is over I hope it put a smile upon yer face,
For to survive in those days, gaun to the pawn wasn't a disgrace.

The Brazen Head

This is a pub you all know well where Celtic supporters meet,
It is at the junction of Cathcart Rd and old Cumberland Street.

The Pub's boss is called Gian and Seamus the Manager true,
While aw the nice barmaids are great at serving you yer brew.

All the punters who drink there are happy and easy to please,
And the name of the pub cleaner is oor ain lovely Lynne Lees.

People do come from miles around to relax drink up and meet,
And when Celtic scores a goal the Brazen jumps up three feet.

Rangers supporters drink in the Sou'wester a pub not far away,
Meeting there cheering on their team each and every Saturday.

These pubs are only a few left cause the Gorbals had so many,
Jist like aw the tenements and shops we're hardly left with any.

So now I've written my poem for us it is written with no self pity,
I remember years ago the Brazen was called the "Granite City".

Wee Bonnies

I went to wee Bonnies Primary, it wiz only one street away,
And got taught all of my lessons by the teacher every day.

Some teachers spoke so harsh others had a voice of silk,
Who can forget the morning time gettin a wee bottle o milk

My favourite was a Mr Jimmy D'arcy he'd be the best of all,
Lessons were soon forgotten when somebody said football.

Playtime wiz magic our running around it jist wouldn't cease,
Well only fur a minute till we'd eaten oor playtime jeely piece.

Lassies playin beds or peever, boys aw playing with a fitbaw,
And if there wiz a fight then the teacher wid lay doon the law.

This was wee Bonnies school and us weans were full of zest,
But if we were naughty teachers' belt gave us six of the best.

Then came the eleven plus exam, oor cheeks were all aglow,
Top marks meant Holyrood, less then to big Bonnies you'd go.

Big Bonnies

Going to big Bonnies in 1960, had my eyes all opened up wide,
Where boys and girls got taught from all over Glesga's soo-side.

The Headmaster was a Mr Berry, the deputy was big Scud Lee,
He'd scud his knuckles off of ma'h heid I went weak at the knee.

Twas here in the classes where us Bonnies pupils did aw amass,
Heading all back to the Gorbals the war cry wiz Cumbie ya bass.

When going to the toilets it could really sometimes be a big joke,
Everyone puffing a Woodbine you couldn't see for aw the smoke.

There was this ritual in the boys playground it stood us all in awe,
If newcomers were spotted they wur thrown over a 6 feet high wa'.

Yes big Bonnies was a springboard for us all in oor later adult life,
Taught us all how to toughen up and deal with oor everyday strife.

So before I end ma'h tale for you there's jist wan thing before I go,
And that is big Bonnies went upmarket and got called John Bosco.

Porridge

You either loved it or loathed it, and that's the honest truth,
Loving each spoonful of it or wantin to spit it oot yer mooth.

My sister sprinkled sugar over it I thought she'd never halt,
While I was totally opposite as over it I would sprinkle salt.

I used to sit and watch my Ma stirring oats into that big pot,
As soon as she poured it into my plate I ate the bloomin lot.

Winter morning's the porridge acted jist like central heating,
Weans that diddny eat porridge had faces always greeting.

Summer months my Ma bought other cereals from the shop,
Either corn flakes or those wans that went snap/crackle/pop.

Got to say I wiz honestly glad, winter came back and nae fibs,
Cause Ma would make the porridge that stuck fast to my ribs.

Ye can buy porridge in packets into the microwave it will go,
But it is not a patch on the stuff Ma made all those years ago.

Saint Francis'

We'd Churches and Chapels in the soo-side to make us go agog,
And for the Jewish Community, there was the odd old synagogue.

But whatever denomination we were or for worship we did meet,
St Francis stood in glory between Mathieston and Sandyfaulds St.

Happy couples got wed there, promising to cherish one another,
Wae Gorbals history bein made as my father married my mother.

What about the May Day procession, the girl crowned May Queen,
How the Gorbals people gathered there it wiz the place to be seen.

St Francis' had a great tradition aw the Brothers there were grand,
The icing on the cake fur us wiz that brilliant St Francis' Pipe Band.

And here lay the bones of St Valentine who looked on lovers sweet,
But they got moved to Blessed John Duns Scotus in Ballater Street.

There's talk about St Francis' to be re-opened as a Chapel one day,
That would be fantastic as parishioners cood once again go to pray.

The Rose Garden

I close my eyes and think back, until my old memory does harden.
When the tenements stood either side of the Gorbals Rose Garden.

To all us weans it wiz the "Rosie," and we played in there fur a dare,
Never really thinking about all the poor souls who were buried there.

It wiz an adventure playground that had a Parky, who wiz never lax,
And right opposite there was the knitwear company called Twomax.

Walking along Rutherglen Road, we'd pass through those gates so neat,
And no far from here wiz where Benny Lynch wiz born, on Florence Street.

But years later the headstones and peoples' remains wiz taken away,
So now we are left with this beautiful Rose Garden, we all enjoy today.

People go and sit while relaxing on the seats which is really so sound,
Not really thinking of its place here as the Gorbals first burial ground.

So many changes to the Gorbals and in Glasgow's mighty Metropolis,
As we think of those poor souls, here and in the Southern Necropolis.

The Square Sausage

Of all the foods I've ever eaten there's one that is my favourite meat,
And people know it as the Lorne sausage, so good it cannot be beat.

Ye can have it with a full Scottish breakfast, laying there on yer plate,
Beside yer egg, beans, tattie scone your square sausage tastes great.

I left Glasgow years ago to go live in London with all its Cafes galore,
But when I asked fur it on a crusty roll, they haddny heard of it before.

All the Cafe owners said we have link sausage which tastes so grand,
Well to be fair to them I tried them, but the taste was oh so very bland.

Worldwide I've tasted all kind of sausages, but they leave me at a loss,
Every day dreaming of the square sausage all covered in broon sauce.

Each year I holiday back in the soo-side, oh it's great to be back hame.
Leaving London far behind, as their sausages jist don't taste the same.

Back again to be with my ain people and that is the God's honest truth,
Canny wait to eat a square sausage, that has me slaverin at the mooth.

Printed in Great Britain
by Amazon